COURSE 3

Practice Workbook

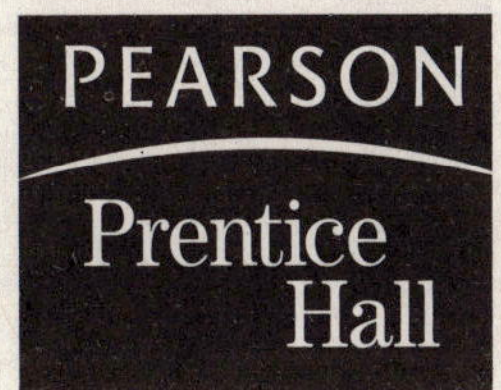

Needham, Massachusetts
Upper Saddle River, New Jersey

ISBN: 0-13-037702-3

3 4 5 6 7 8 9 10   07 06 05

Practice Workbook

Contents

Answers appear in the back of each Chapter Support File.

Contents (cont.)

Practice 1-1

Algebraic Expressions and the Order of Operations

Write an algebraic expression for each word phrase.

1. 5 less than a number _______________

2. 15 more than the absolute value of a number _______________

3. the product of a number and -8 _______________

4. 5 more than a number, divided by 9 _______________

5. 3 more than the product of 8 and a number _______________

6. 3 less than the absolute value of a number, times 4 _______________

Write an algebraic expression for each situation. Explain what the variable represents.

7. the amount of money Waldo has if he has $10 more than Jon

8. the amount of money that Mika has if she has some quarters

9. how much weight Kirk can lift if he lifts 30 lb more than his brother

10. how fast Rya runs if she runs 5 mi/h slower than Danae

Write a word phrase that can be represented by each variable expression.

11. $n \div (4)$

12. $n + 4$

13. $3n$

14. $n - 8$

Evaluate each expression for $n = 2$, $x = 6$, and $y = 4$.

15. $11x + 7$ _______________

16. $29y - 15$ _______________

17. $6(n + 8)$ _______________

18. $(24 \div x) + 18$ _______________

19. $(x + n) \div y$ _______________

20. $xn + y$ _______________

21. $(6 \cdot 8 + y) \cdot n$ _______________

22. $6(8 + y) \cdot n$ _______________

23. $6 \cdot 8 + y \cdot n$ _______________

24. $y + n \cdot n$ _______________

25. $12 \div x + xy$ _______________

26. $(2n + 2y) \div 2x$ _______________

27. $n + x(y + 1)$ _______________

28. $y \div n \cdot 3x$ _______________

29. $4 + x \div n + 2$ _______________

30. $4n + x(y + 1)$ _______________

Practice 1-2

Problem Solving: Use a Problem-Solving Plan

Use the problem-solving plan to solve each problem.

1. Philip drove 1,096 miles in two days. He drove 240 miles more on the second day than he drove on the first day. How many miles did he drive each day?

   ____

2. Bea raised some cows and some turkeys. She raised a total of 28 cows and turkeys. There were 96 legs in all. How many cows and how many turkeys did Bea raise?

   ____

3. Two integers have a difference of -11 and a sum of -3. What are the integers?

   ____

4. Tickets for a benefit dinner were on sale for three weeks. Twice as many tickets were sold during the third week as were sold during the first two weeks combined. If a total of 1,095 tickets were sold, how many were sold the third week?

   ____

Choose a problem-solving method to solve each problem. Show all your work.

5. Priya ordered twice as many blankets as she did quilts for the department store where she works. The order was for 126 items. How many blankets and how many quilts did Priya order?

   ____

6. Kent is three years older than his sister Debbie. The sum of their ages is 105. Find their ages.

   ____

7. A bowling league has 16 teams. During a single-elimination tournament, the winner of each match goes on to the next round. How many matches does the winning team need to play?

   ____

8. In the addition problems below, each letter represents the same digit in both problems. Replace each letter with a different digit, 1 through 9, so that both addition problems are true. (There are two possible answers.)

```
  A B C        A D G
+ D E F      + B E H
-------      -------
  G H I        C F I
```

Practice 1-3

Write an integer to represent each situation.

1. The top of the world's lowest known active volcano is 160 ft below sea level.

   ____

2. The football team gained three yards on a play.

   ____

3. Jenni owes her friend $20.

   ____

4. The temperature yesterday was five degrees above zero.

   ____

Use the information in the graph at the right for questions 5–8.

5. The highest outdoor temperature ever recorded in Nevada, 122°F, was recorded on June 23, 1954. Was it ever that hot in Idaho? Explain.

   ____

   ____

6. Which state had a recorded high temperature of 134°F?

   ____

7. The lowest temperature ever recorded in Maine, −48°F, was recorded on January 17, 1925. Was it ever that cold in Minnesota? Explain.

   ____

   ____

8. Which state on the graph had a recorded low temperature of 60°F below zero?

   ____

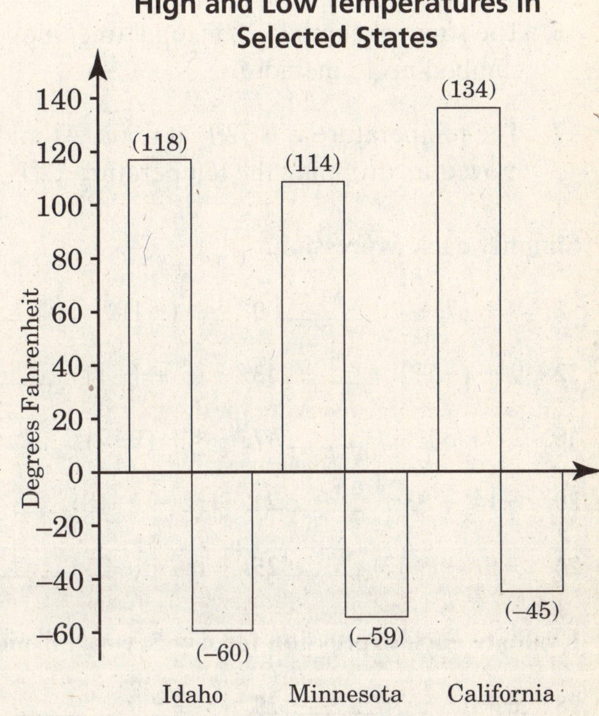

Compare. Write >, <, or =.

9. -12 ☐ 10

10. 9 ☐ -12

11. $|4|$ ☐ $|-9|$

12. $|26|$ ☐ $|-26|$

13. $|42|$ ☐ $|-93|$

14. 53 ☐ -21

15. $|6|$ ☐ 0

16. $|9|$ ☐ $|-13|$

Order the integers in each set from least to greatest.

17. $0, -5, 5, -15, 15, 25, -25$

    ____

18. $6, -4, -8, 3, 1, -2, 7$

    ____

19. $27, -10, -6, -18, 3, 9, -8$

    ____

20. $-3, -7, 7, 4, -9, -4, -1$

    ____

Practice 1-4 Adding and Subtracting Integers

Write the addition equation that is suggested by each model.

1. 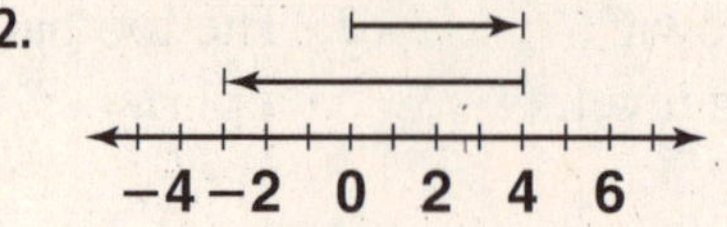

2.

3. 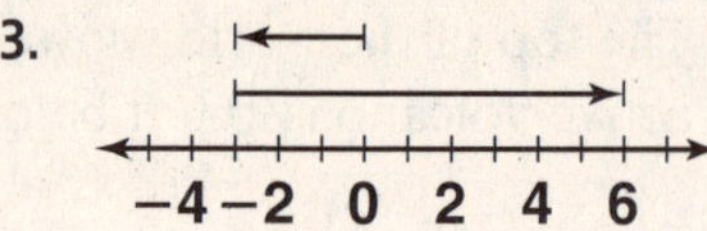

________________   ________________   ________________

Write an algebraic expression to find the sum for each situation.

4. The varsity football team gained 7 yd on one play and then lost 4 yd. _______________

5. The airplane descended 140 ft and then rose 112 ft. _______________

6. The squirrel climbed 18 in. up a tree, slipped back 4 in., and then climbed up 12 in. more. _______________

7. The temperature was 72°F at noon. At midnight a cold front moved in, dropping the temperature 12°F. _______________

Simplify each expression.

8. $8 + (7)$ _______ **9.** $9 + (-4)$ _______ **10.** $-6 + (-8)$ _______ **11.** $8 + (-14)$ _______

12. $9 + (-17)$ _______ **13.** $-15 + (-11)$ _______ **14.** $-23 + 18$ _______ **15.** $-19 + 16$ _______

16. $27 + 34$ _______ **17.** $-8 + (-17)$ _______ **18.** $19 + (-8)$ _______ **19.** $23 + (-31)$ _______

20. $-14 - 33$ _______ **21.** $-32 - (-18)$ _______ **22.** $-15 - (-26)$ _______ **23.** $32 - (-16)$ _______

24. $-19 - (-12)$ _______ **25.** $-16 - (-21)$ _______ **26.** $27 - 19$ _______ **27.** $-14 - 27$ _______

Evaluate each expression for $x = 5$, $y = -6$, and $z = -7$.

28. $x + y$ _______ **29.** $15 - z$ _______ **30.** $y - z$ _______ **31.** $x + y - z$ _______

32. $y - 15 + x$ _______ **33.** $32 - z + x$ _______ **34.** $|x| - |y|$ _______ **35.** $z + |x|$ _______

36. Jill and Joe are playing a game. The chart at the right shows the points gained or lost on each round.

  a. Who has the most points after the fifth round?

  ____

  b. To win, a player must have 20 points. How many points does each player need to win?

  ____

Round	Jill	Joe
1	10	12
2	−2	3
3	6	−8
4	4	0
5	−2	7

Practice 1-5

Find each product or quotient.

1. $-4 \cdot 8$

2. $-7 \cdot (-9)$

3. $-5 \cdot (-11)$

4. $20 \cdot (-3)$

5. $2(-3)(-3)$

6. $(-4)(-4)(-4)$

7. $(-3)(4)(-5)$

8. $(5)(2)(-20)$

9. $-63 \div 7$

10. $81 \div (-9)$

11. $-77 \div 7$

12. $96 \div (-12)$

13. $-54 \div (-6)$

14. $-120 \div 10$

15. $-1{,}000 \div (-100)$

16. $540 \div (-90)$

17. The value of Jim's telephone calling card decreases 15 cents for every minute he uses it. Yesterday he used the card to make a 6-minute call. How much did the value of the card change?

18. One day the temperature in Lone Grove, Oklahoma fell 3 degrees per hour for 5 consecutive hours. Give the total change in temperature.

19. The population of New Orleans, Lousiana, decreased from about 558,000 in 1980 to 497,000 in 1990. On average, about how much did the population change *each year*?

You want to find a route from Start to Finish. Evaluate the expression in each square. You can only move to the right or down, and you can only move to a square that has an answer greater than the expression in your current square. Draw a line through the route you will take.

Start

$-9(26)$	$-29 - 146$	$-25 + (-100)$	$-9(40)$	$8(7)$	$23 + (-9)$
$-10(27)$	$-800 - 92$	$200 \div (-2)$	$-40 + 12$	$-600 \div 6$	$21(16)$
$-26 - 19$	$-90 - 15$	$400 \div (-2)$	$17 - 19$	$-4(8)$	$200 \div 4$
$-17 - (-24)$	$17(11)$	$500 \div (-4)$	$5(0)$	$8 - (-27)$	$47 + 1$

Finish

Practice 1-6

Using Integers with Mean, Median, and Mode

Find the mean, median, and mode of each data set.

1. hours of piano practice

____

Hours Mr. Capelli's students practice

2 1 2 0 1 2 2 1 2 2

2. days of snow per month

____

Monthly snow days in Central City

8 10 5 1 0 0 0 0 0 1 3 12

3. number of students per class

____

Class size in Westmont Middle School

32 26 30 35 25 24 35 30 29 25

4. ratings given by students to a new movie

____

Student ratings of a movie

10 9 10 8 9 7 5 3 8 9 9 10 9 9 7

5. points scored in five basketball games

____

Points scored by Westmont JV

72 67 83 92 54

6. account balance for one month

____

Monthly balance for the last five months

$129   −$136   −$201 $146   −$154

Is the mean, median, or mode the best measure of central tendency for each type of data? Explain.

7. most popular movie in the past month

____

8. favorite hobby

____

9. class size in a school

____

10. ages of members in a club

____

Each person has taken four tests and has one more test to take. Find the score that each person must make to change the mean or median as shown.

11. Barry has scores of 93, 84, 86, and 75. He wants to raise the mean to 86.

____

12. Liz has scores of 87, 75, 82, and 93. She wants to raise the median to 87.

____

13. Jim has scores of 60, 73, 82, and 75. He wants to raise the mean to 75.

____

14. Andrea has scores of 84, 73, 92, and 88. She wants the median to be 86.

____

Practice 1-7

Powers and Exponents

Write using exponents.

1. $8 \cdot 8 \cdot 8 \cdot 8 \cdot 8$ **2.** $(-2)(-2)(-2)(-2)$ **3.** $x \cdot x \cdot x \cdot x \cdot x \cdot x$

4. $(-3m)(-3m)(-3m)$ **5.** $4 \cdot t \cdot t \cdot t$ **6.** $(5v)(5v)(5v)(5v)(5v)$

Write each expression as a product of the same factor.

7. a^2 _________________________   **8.** 19^3 _________________________

9. -6^2 _________________________   **10.** $-x^3$ _________________________

11. $(-5)^4$ _________________________   **12.** 4^3 _________________________

13. $-(10)^2$ _________________________   **14.** 20^1 _________________________

Simplify each expression.

15. $(-4)^2 + 10 \cdot 2$ _________   **16.** $-4^2 + 10 \cdot 2$ _________   **17.** $(5 \cdot 3)^2 + 8$ _________

18. $5 \cdot 3^2 + 8$ _________   **19.** $9 + (7 - 4)^2$ _________   **20.** $-9 + 7 - 4^2$ _________

21. $(-6)^2 + 3^3 - 7$ **22.** $-6^2 + 3^3 - 7$ **23.** $2^3 + (8 - 5) \cdot 4 - 5^2$

24. $(2^3 + 8) - 5 \cdot 4 - 5^2$ **25.** $2^3 \cdot 3 - 5 \cdot 5^2 + 8$ **26.** $2^3 \cdot 3 - 5(5^2 + 8)$

Evaluate each expression for the given value.

27. $4x^2$ for $x = 3$ **28.** $(5b)^2$ for $b = 2$ **29.** $-6x^2$ for $x = 3$ **30.** $(-3g)^2$ for $g = 2$

Estimate the value of each expression.

31. $7 + 3q; q = 7.6$ **32.** $j^2 + 6; j = 4.7$ **33.** $2m^2 - 3m; m = 1.6$

34. $y^2 - 19y + 16; y = 2.5$ **35.** $x^2 + 7x - 19; x = 4.21$ **36.** $v^2 + v; v = 9.8$

37. Suppose you own a card shop. You buy one line of cards at a rate of
4 cards for \$5. You plan to sell the cards at a rate of 3 cards for \$5.
How many cards must you sell in order to make a profit of \$100.

Practice 1-8

Properties of Numbers

Use mental math to simplify each expression.

1. $8 + (-2) + 7 + (-5)$

2. $-7 + 9 + 11 + (-13)$

3. $17 + (-9) + 18 + (-11)$

4. $65 + 23 + 35$

5. $220 + 343 + 80$

6. $230 + 170 + 18 + (-5)$

7. $(-5)(38)(-20)$

8. $2 \cdot 83 \cdot (-5)$

9. $-5 \cdot (2 \cdot 38)$

10. $4 \cdot (25 \cdot 27)$

11. $(50)(86)(20)$

12. $-4 \cdot (36 \cdot 5)$

Use mental math and the Distributive Property to simplify.

13. $25(-99)$ _______

14. $19(-6)$ _______

15. $6 \cdot \$2.99$ _______

16. $102 \cdot \$21$ _______

17. $19 \cdot 21$ _______

18. $26 \cdot 97$ _______

19. $21 \cdot (-11)$ _______

20. $9 \cdot \$4.98$ _______

21. $103 \cdot \$32$ _______

Determine whether each equation is true or false.

22. $9 \cdot 8 + 6 = 9 \cdot 6 + 8$

23. $-7(11 - 4) = 7(15)$

24. $12 \cdot 7 = 10 \cdot 7 + 2 \cdot 7$

25. $15 + (-17) = -17 + 15$

26. $93 \cdot (-8) = -93 \cdot 8$

27. $53 + (-19) = -53 + 19$

The table to the right shows changes in daily temperature over a 5-day period.

28. Which two-day period had the greatest change in temperature?

29. On Sunday the temperature was 20°F. What was the temperature at the end of the day on Friday?

Day	Change in Temperature
Mon	−12°F
Tues	+6°F
Wed	−4°F
Thurs	−9°F
Fri	+8°F

Practice 2-1

Solving One-Step Equations

Solve each equation. Check the solution.

1. $x - 6 = -18$

2. $-14 = 8 + j$

3. $4.19 + w = 19.72$

4. $b + \frac{1}{6} = \frac{7}{8}$

5. $9 + k = 27$

6. $14 + t = -17$

7. $v - 2.59 = 26$

8. $r + 9 = 15$

9. $n - 19 = 26$

10. $14 = -3 + s$

11. $9 = d - 4.3$

12. $g - \frac{1}{4} = \frac{5}{8}$

13. $\frac{a}{-6} = 2$

14. $18 = \frac{v}{-1.8}$

15. $46 = 2.3m$

16. $-114 = -6k$

17. $0 = \frac{b}{19}$

18. $136 = 8y$

19. $0.6j = -1.44$

20. $\frac{q}{7.4} = 8.3$

21. $28b = -131.6$

22. $\frac{n}{-9} = -107$

23. $37c = -777$

24. $\frac{n}{-1.28} = 4.96$

Write and solve an equation for each situation.

25. Yesterday Josh sold some boxes of greeting cards. Today he sold seven boxes. If he sold 25 boxes in all, how many did he sell yesterday?

26. Skylar bought seven books at $12.95 each. How much did Skylar spend?

27. After Simon donated four books to the school library, he had 28 books left. How many books did Simon have to start with?

28. Eugenio has five payments left to make on his computer. If each payment is $157.90, how much does he still owe?

Practice 2-2

Solving Two-Step Equations

Solve each equation.

1. $4r + 6 = 14$

2. $9y - 11 = 7$

3. $\frac{m}{4} + 6 = 3$

4. $\frac{k}{-9} + 6 = -4$

5. $-5b - 6 = -11$

6. $\frac{v}{-7} + 8 = 19$

7. $3.4t + 19.36 = -10.22$

8. $\frac{n}{-1.6} + 7.9 = 8.4$

9. $4.6b + 26.8 = 50.72$

10. $\frac{a}{-8.06} + 7.02 = 18.4$

11. $-2.06d + 18 = -10.84$

12. $\frac{e}{-95} + 6 = 4$

13. $-9i - 17 = -26$

14. $\frac{j}{-1.9} + 2.7 = -8.6$

15. $14.9 = 8.6 + 0.9m$

16. $84 = 19 + \frac{z}{12}$

17. $15w - 21 = -111$

18. $-12.4 = -19.1 + \frac{n}{-7.9}$

19. Hugo received $100 for his birthday. He then saved $20 per week until he had a total of $460 to buy a printer. Use an equation to show how many weeks it took him to save the money.

20. A health club charges a $50 initial fee plus $2 for each visit. Moselle has spent a total of $144 at the health club this year. Use an equation to find how many visits she has made.

Solve each equation to find the value of the variable. Write the answer in the puzzle. Do not include any negative signs or any decimals.

ACROSS

1. $6n - 12 = 2.4$

2. $\frac{n}{3} + 4.6 = 21.6$

4. $x - 3 = 51.29$

6. $2z + 2 = 7.6$

DOWN

1. $\frac{j}{5} - 14 = -9$

2. $3x - 2 = 169$

3. $\frac{x}{4} + 1 = 19$

4. $\frac{x}{3} + 4 = 22$

5. $2x - 2 = 182$

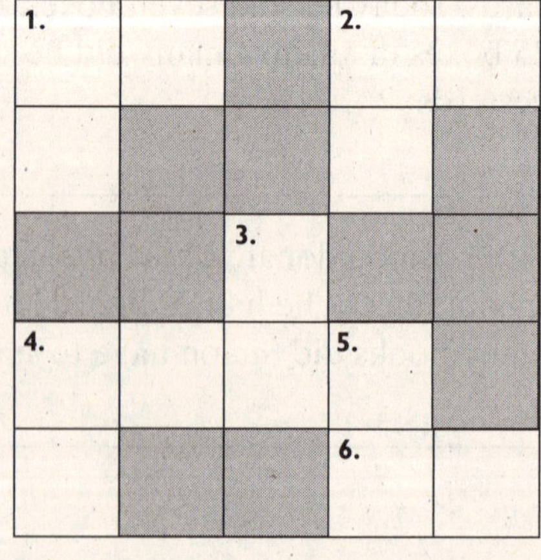

Practice 2-3

Simplifying Algebraic Expressions

Simplify each expression.

1. $4a + 7 + 2a$

2. $8(k - 9)$

3. $5n + 6n - 2n$

4. $(w + 3)7$

5. $5(b - 6) + 9$

6. $-4 + 8(2 + t)$

7. $-4 + 3(6 + k)$

8. $12j - 9j$

9. $6(d - 8)$

10. $-9 + 8(x + 6)$

11. $4(m + 6) - 3$

12. $27 + 2(f - 19)$

13. $4v - 7 + 8v + 4 - 5$

14. $5(g + 8) + 7 + 4g$

15. $12h - 17 - h + 16 - 2h$

16. $7(e - 8) + 12 - 2e$

17. $-3y + 7 + y + 6y$

18. $(3.2m + 1.8) - 1.07m$

Simplify each expression.

19. $28k + 36(7 + k)$

20. $3.09(j + 4.6)$

21. $12b + 24(b - 42)$

22. $7.9y + 8.4 - 2.04y$

23. $4.3(5.6 + c)$

24. $83x + 15(x - 17)$

25. $9.8c + 8d - 4.6c + 2.9d$

26. $18 + 27m - 29 + 36m$

27. $8(j + 12) + 4(k - 19)$

28. $4.2r + 8.1s + 1.09r + 6.32s$

29. $43 + 16c - 18d + 56c + 16d$

30. $9(a + 14) + 8(b - 16)$

31. Tyrone bought 15.3 gal of gasoline priced at g dollars per gal, 2 qt of oil priced at q dollars per qt, and a wiper blade priced at $3.79. Write an expression that represents the total cost of these items.

32. Choose a number. Multiply by 2. Add 6 to the product. Divide by 2. Then subtract 3. What is the answer? Repeat this process using two different numbers. Explain.

Practice 2-4   **Solving Multi-Step Equations**

Solve each equation. Check the solution.

1. $2(2.5b - 9) + 6b = -7$

2. $12y = 2y + 40$

3. $6(c + 4) = 4c - 18$

4. $0.7w + 16 + 4w = 27.28$

5. $24 = -6(m + 1) + 18$

6. $0.5m + 6.4 = 4.9 - 0.1m$

7. $7k - 8 + 2(k + 12) = 52$

8. $14b = 16(b + 12)$

9. $4(1.5c + 6) - 2c = -9$

10. $7y = y - 42$

11. $9(d - 4) = 5d + 8$

12. $0.5n + 17 + n = 20$

13. $20 = -4(f + 6) + 14$

14. $12j = 16(j - 8)$

15. $0.7p + 4.6 = 7.3 - 0.2p$

16. $9a - 4 + 3(a - 11) = 23$

17. $6(f + 5) = 2f - 8$

18. $15p = 6(p - 9)$

19. $0.5t + 4.1 = 5.7 - 0.3t$

20. $9q - 14 + 3(q - 8) = 7$

21. A banquet is planned for 50 people. The caterer charges $1,500 for the food. How much is that per person? Write an equation and solve.

22. Stephanie is six years old. She is one year older than one-sixth the age of her mother. How old is Stephanie's mother? Write an equation and solve.

Practice 2-5

Problem Solving: Draw a Diagram and Write an Equation

Solve each problem by either drawing a diagram or writing an equation. Explain why you chose the method you did.

1. The cost of a long-distance phone call is $.56 for the first minute and $.32 for each additional minute. What was the total length of a call that cost $9.20?

2. An elevator started on the 7th floor. It went up 6 floors, down 4 floors, up 9 floors, and down 5 floors. On what floor did the elevator finally stop?

3. Two cars start at the same point, at the same time, and travel in opposite directions. In how many hours will the cars be 232 miles apart if the slower car travels at 26 mi/h, and the faster car travels at 32 mi/h?

Use any strategy to solve each problem. Show your work.

4. Mary and Jim have tickets to a concert. Mary's ticket number is one less than Jim's ticket number. The product of their numbers is 812. What are the two numbers?

5. The Beards' budget is shown at the right. Their house payment is raised $120. Their income will be no more than it is now, so they plan on subtracting an equal amount from each of the other categories. How much will be available to spend on bills?

Beards' Budget

Item	Amount
House	$650
Food	$300
Bills	$250
Other	$140

6. Antonio watches $\frac{2}{3}$ of a movie at home and then decides to finish watching it later. If he already has watched 2 hours of the movie, how long is it?

Practice 2-6

Solving Inequalities by Adding or Subtracting

Write an inequality for each graph.

1. 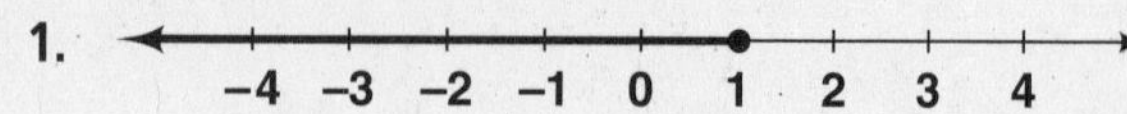

____

2. 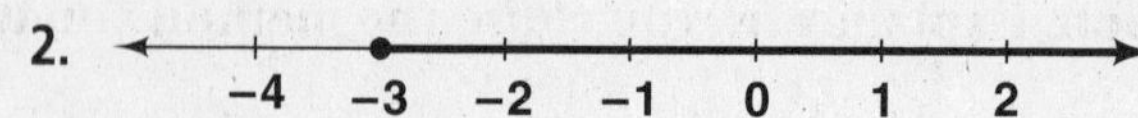

____

3. 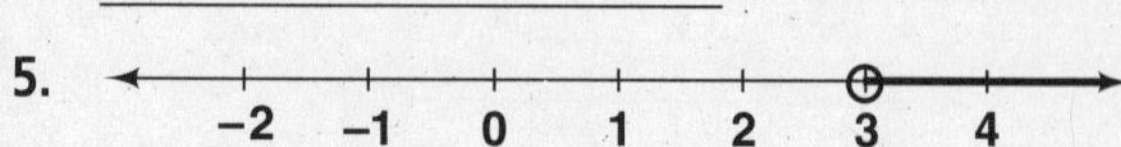

____

4. 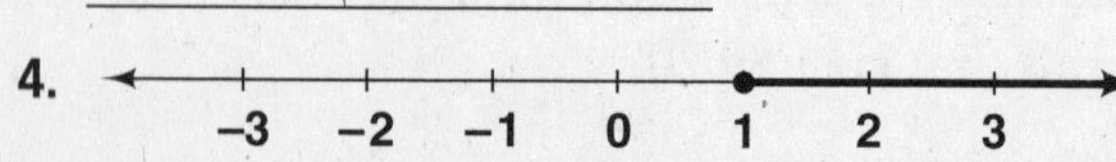

____

5. 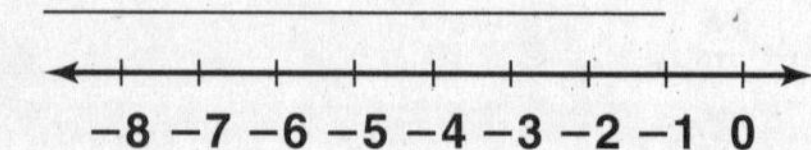

____

Graph each inequality on a number line.

6. $x \geq -6$

7. $x < -5$

8. $x \leq 0$

9. $x \leq 7$

10. $x < 5$

Solve each inequality. Graph the solutions.

11. $m + 6 > 2$

12. $q + 4 \leq 9$

13. $w - 6 > -9$

14. $y - 3 < -4$

15. $k + 9 \leq 12$

16. $u + 6 \geq 8$

Write and solve an inequality to answer each question.

17. The amount of snow on the ground increased by 8 in. between 7 P.M. and 10 P.M. By 10 P.M., there was less than 2 ft of snow. How much snow was there by 7 P.M.?

____

18. The school record for points scored in a basketball season by one player is 462. Maria has 235 points so far this season. How many more points does she need to break the record?

____

Practice 2-7

Solving Inequalities by Multiplying and Dividing

Solve each inequality and graph the solutions.

1. $-5m < 20$

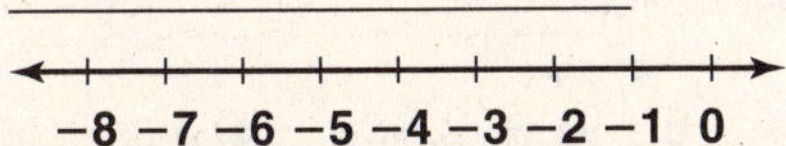

2. $\dfrac{j}{6} \le 0$

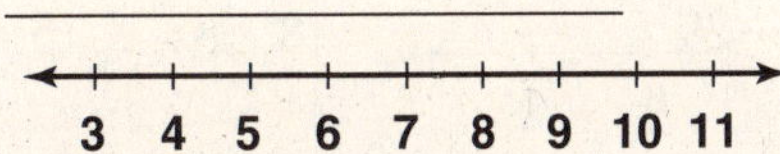

3. $4v > 16$

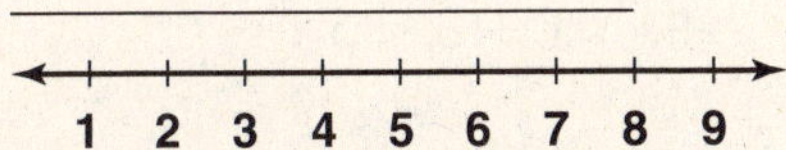

4. $\dfrac{b}{2} < 4$

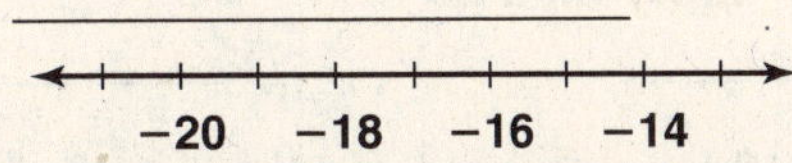

5. $5a > -10$

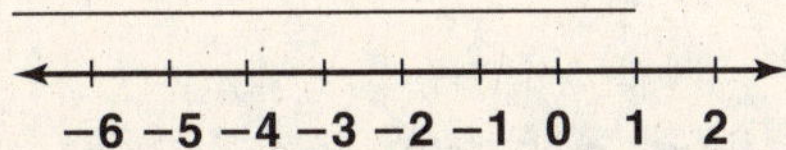

6. $\dfrac{c}{-3} \ge 6$

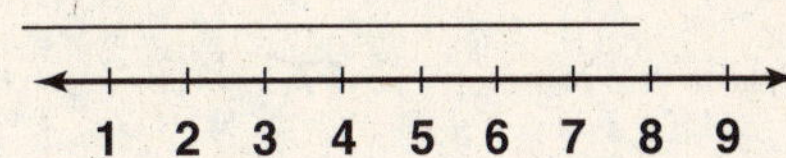

7. $\dfrac{c}{-6} > 1$

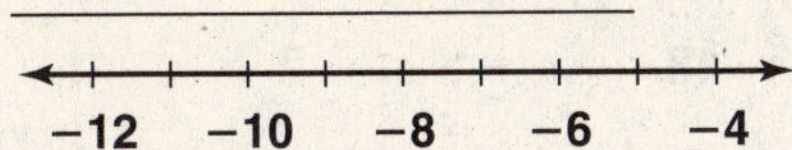

8. $-4i \le -16$

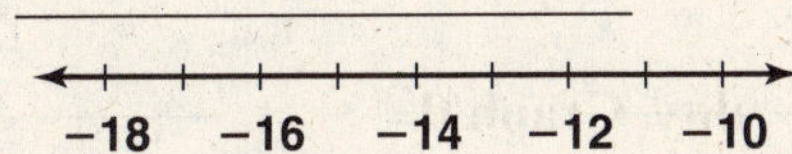

9. $5d < -75$

10. $\dfrac{d}{12} < -1$

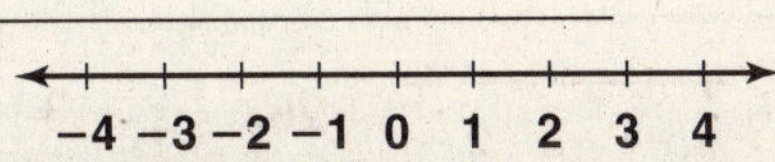

11. $0.5n \ge -2.5$

12. $\dfrac{p}{0.2} \le 10$

Write an inequality for each problem. Solve the inequality. Then give the solution to the problem.

13. Dom wants to buy 5 baseballs. He has $20. What is the most each baseball can cost?

____

14. A typing service charges $5.00 per page. Mrs. Garza does not want to spend more than $50 for the typing. What is the maximum number of pages she can have typed?

____

15. The tables at a restaurant can each seat 8 people. A dinner at the restaurant will be attended by 125 people. How many tables does the restaurant need in order for every person at the dinner to have a seat?

____

Practice 2-8

Solving Two-Step Inequalities

Solve each inequality.

1. $6x + 5 \leq -19$ **2.** $2x + 12 < 24$ **3.** $15x - 9 > 21$

4. $5x - 11 \geq -36$ **5.** $18x - 6 \geq 84$ **6.** $9x + 2.3 > -10.3$

7. $11x + 4 \leq -29$ **8.** $8x + 15 < 71$ **9.** $\frac{1}{2}x + 3 < 5$

10. $\frac{x}{6} - 7 \leq 3$ **11.** $\frac{1}{4}x + 10 > -7$ **12.** $\frac{x}{9} - 15 \geq 5$

13. $12x + 7 \geq 139$ **14.** $3x - 8 \leq 55$ **15.** $7x - 5.8 > 13.1$

16. $4x + 13 < 61$ **17.** $\frac{x}{8} - 7 > -12$ **18.** $\frac{1}{5}x + 8 < -2$

19. $\frac{n}{11} + 2 \leq 6$ **20.** $\frac{x}{7} - 9 \geq -4$ **21.** $20n - 2 \leq 138$

22. $10x - 3 \geq -83$ **23.** $8x - 3.2 > 37.6$ **24.** $12x - 10 > -130$

25. $\frac{w}{10} - 11 > 6$ **26.** $\frac{1}{3}x + 3 < -9$ **27.** $\frac{u}{12} + 4 \leq 8$

Write and solve an inequality to answer each question.

28. A drama club's production of "Oklahoma!" is going to cost $1,250 to produce. How many tickets will they need to sell for $8 each in order to make a profit of at least $830?

29. A pet store is selling hamsters for $3.50 each if you purchase a cage for $18.25. You have at most $30 you can spend. How many hamsters can you buy?

Practice 3-1

Name the coordinates of each point in the graph.

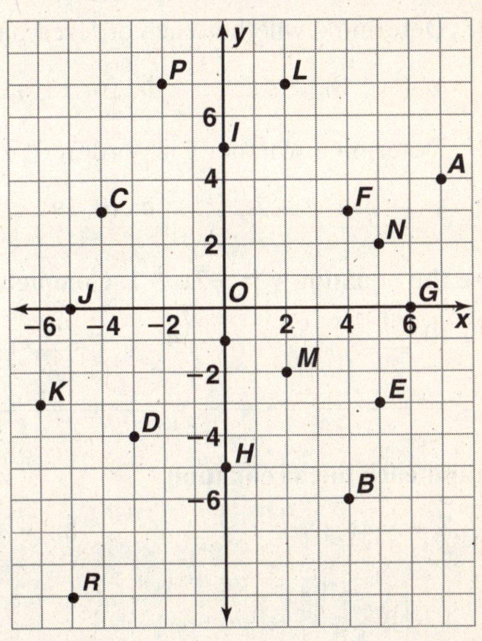

1. J

____

2. R

____

3. K

____

4. M

____

5. I

____

6. P

____

7. N

____

8. L

____

In which quadrant or on which axis is each point located?

9. $(-3, -2)$

____

10. $(7, 0)$

____

11. $(4, 0)$

____

12. $(-3, -9)$

____

13. $(4, -7)$

____

14. $(7, -5)$

____

15. $(2, 9)$

____

16. $(0, 9)$

____

17. $(0, -6)$

____

18. $(4, 2)$

____

19. $(-3, 2)$

____

20. $(0, 0)$

____

21. Arnie plotted points on the graph below. He placed his pencil point at A. He can move either right or down any number of units until he reaches point B. In how many ways can he do this?

____

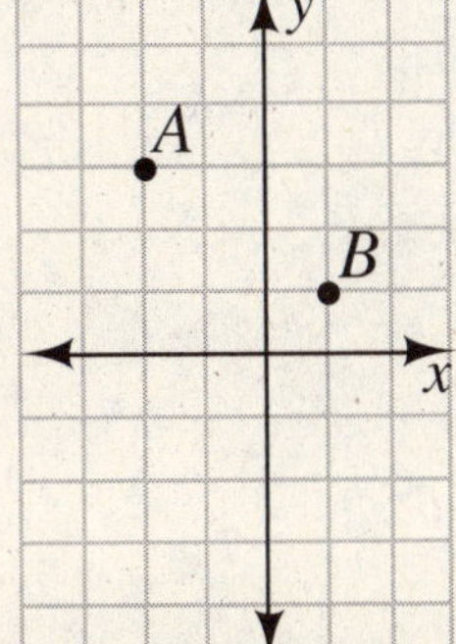

22. Marika had to draw $\triangle ABC$ that fit several requirements.

a. It must fit in the box shown.

b. The side $\overline{AB}$ has coordinates $A(-2, 0)$ and $B(2, 0)$.

c. Point C must be on the y-axis.

Name all the points that could be point C.

____

____

Practice 3-2

Graphing Equations with Two Variables

1. Determine whether each ordered pair is a solution of $y = 3x - 8$.

   a. $(0, -8)$ _______   **b.** $(6, -10)$ _______   **c.** $(-2, -2)$ _______   **d.** $(4, 4)$ _______

2. Determine whether each ordered pair is a solution of $y = -5x + 19$.

   a. $(-3, 4)$ _______   **b.** $(0, 19)$ _______   **c.** $(2, 9)$ _______   **d.** $(-4, 39)$ _______

Use the equation $y = -2x + 1$. Complete each solution.

3. $(0, \underline{\ ?\ })$ 4. $(-5, \underline{\ ?\ })$ 5. $(20, \underline{\ ?\ })$ 6. $(-68, \underline{\ ?\ })$

____________   ____________   ____________   ____________

Graph each linear equation.

7. $y = -4x + 6$

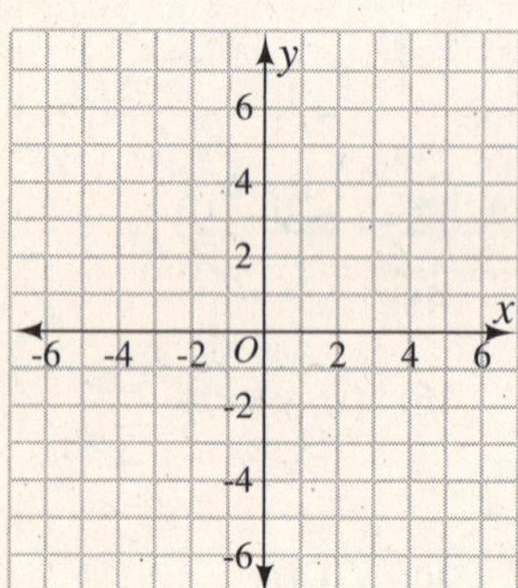

8. $y = \frac{5}{2}x - 5$

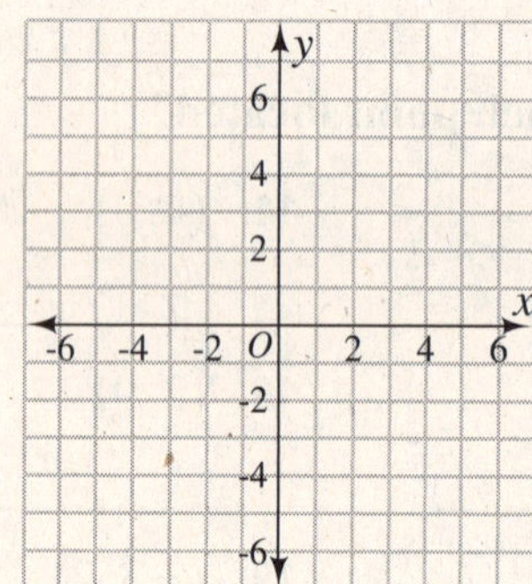

9. $y = -\frac{1}{2}x + 3$

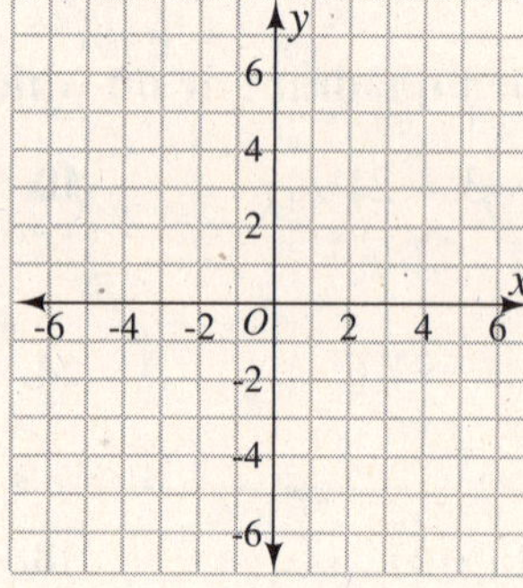

10. $y = \frac{1}{2}x - \frac{1}{2}$

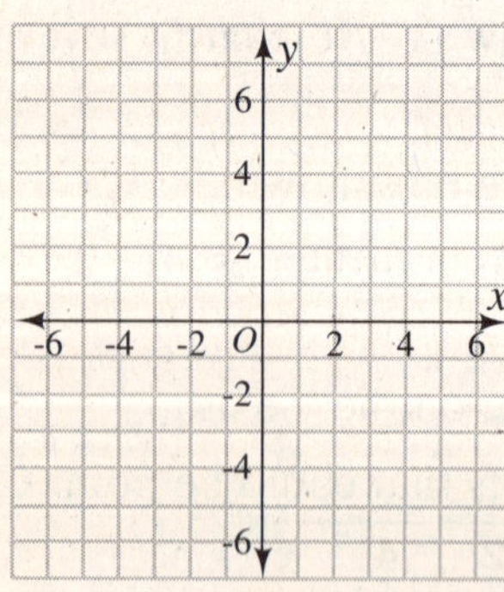

11. $y = -2x + 7$

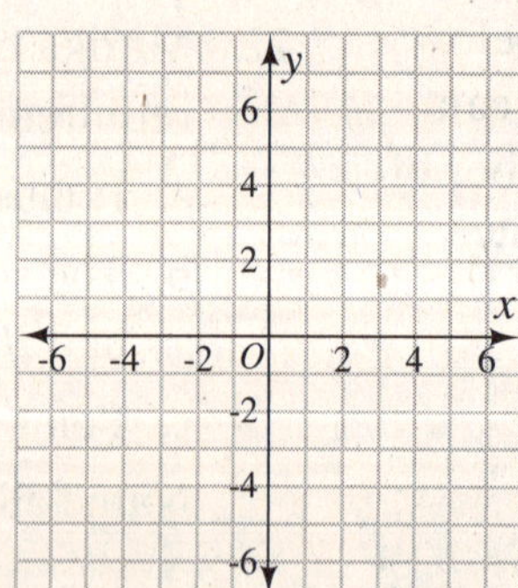

12. $y = -3x - 1$

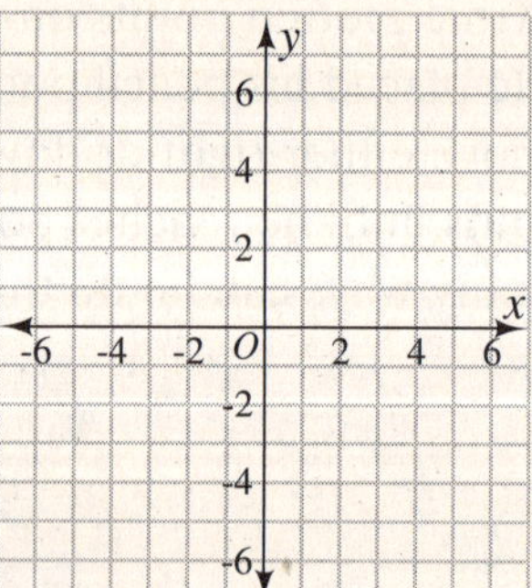

13. Jan wants to buy both maps and atlases for her trip. The maps cost \$2 each, and the atlases cost \$5 each. If she spends \$25 and buys 3 atlases, how many maps can she buy?

____

14. Grapefruits cost \$.65 each and oranges cost \$.20 each. If Keiko spends \$5 and buys 25 \$.20 oranges, how many grapefruits can she buy?

____

Practice 3-3

Understanding Slope

Find the slope of each line.

1. 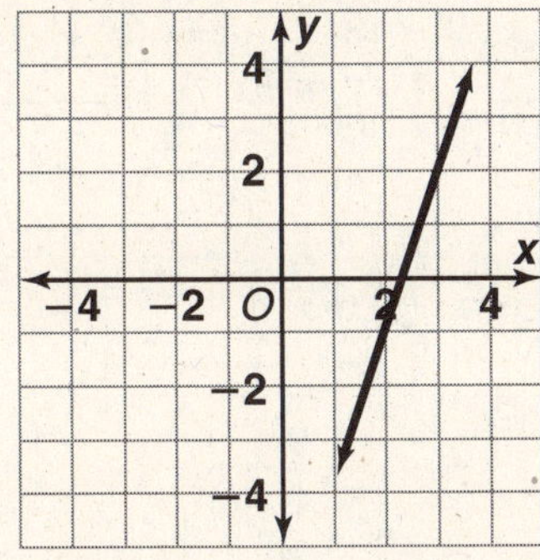

____

2. 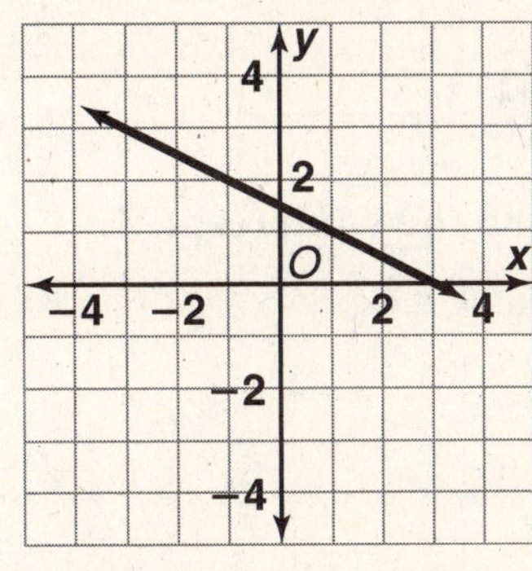

____

3. 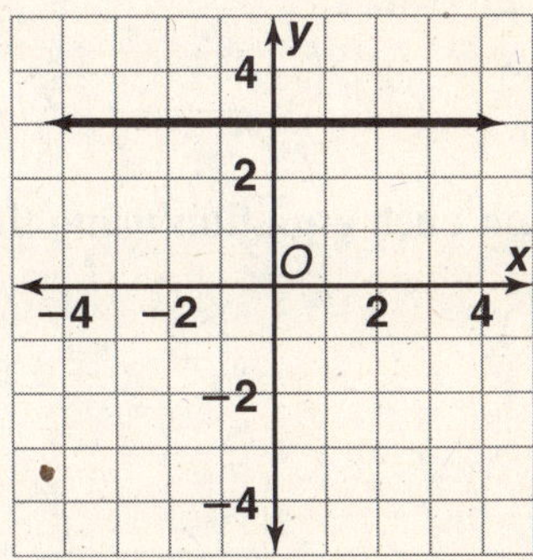

____

4. 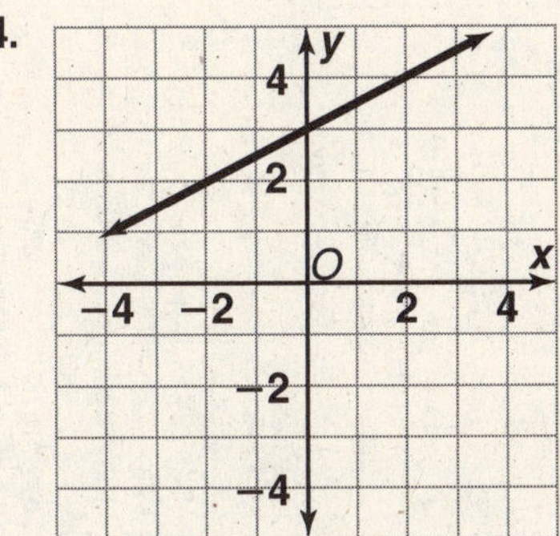

____

5. 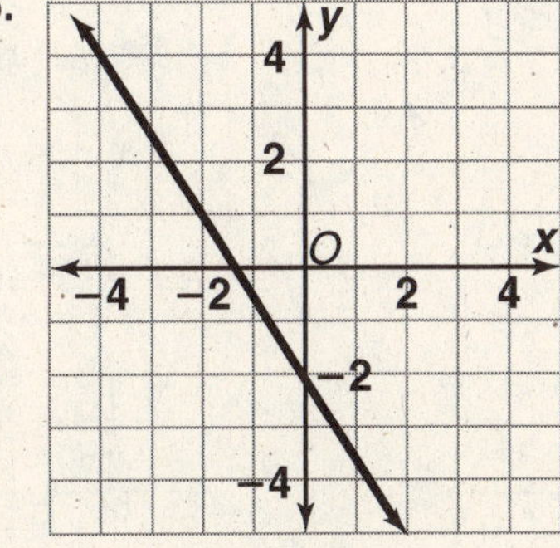

____

The points from each table lie on a line.
Use the table to find the slope of each line.
Then graph the line

6.

x	0	1	2	3	4
y	-3	-1	1	3	5

slope = _________

7.

x	0	1	2	3	4
y	5	3	1	-1	-3

slope = _________

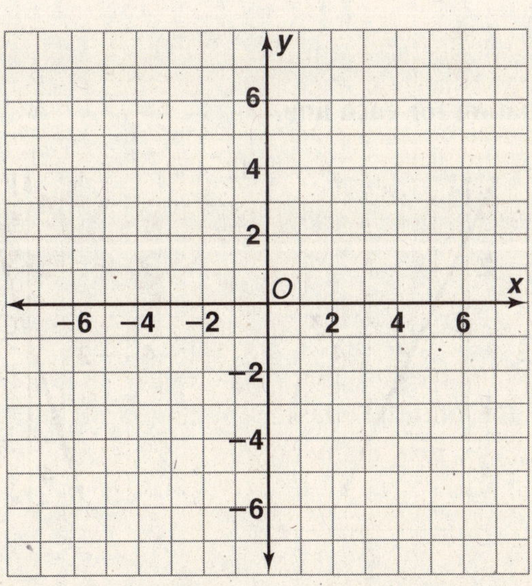

Practice 3-4

Using the *y*-Intercept

Determine if the equation has the same slope as the equation
$y = 2x - 4.$

1. $y = 2x + 4$ _______   **2.** $y = -2x + 3$ _______   **3.** $y = 4x - 2$ _______   **4.** $y = 3x - 4$ _______

Graph each equation using the slope and the *y*-intercept.

5. $y = \frac{3}{4}x - 3$

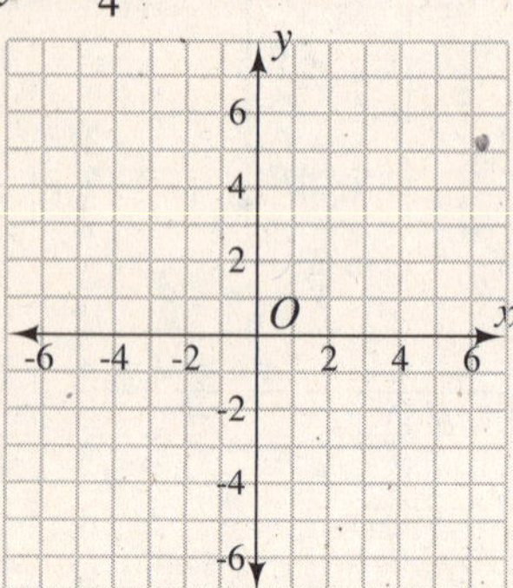

6. $y = -\frac{2}{5}x + 2$

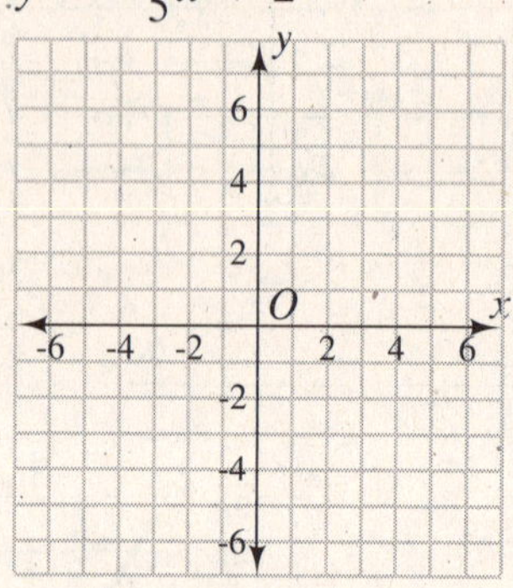

7. $y = -\frac{4}{3}x + 4$

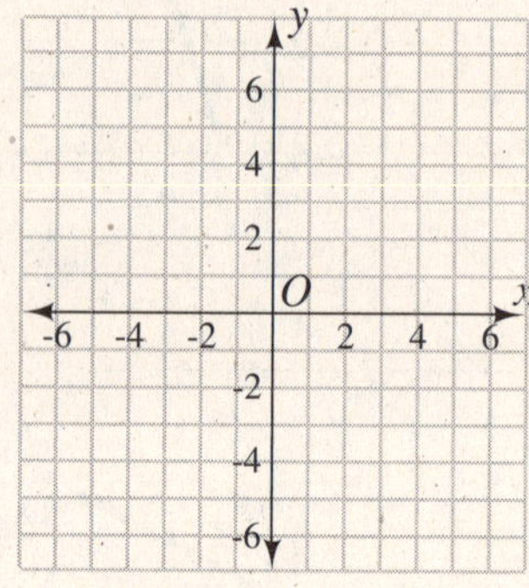

8. $y = \frac{4}{5}x + 4$

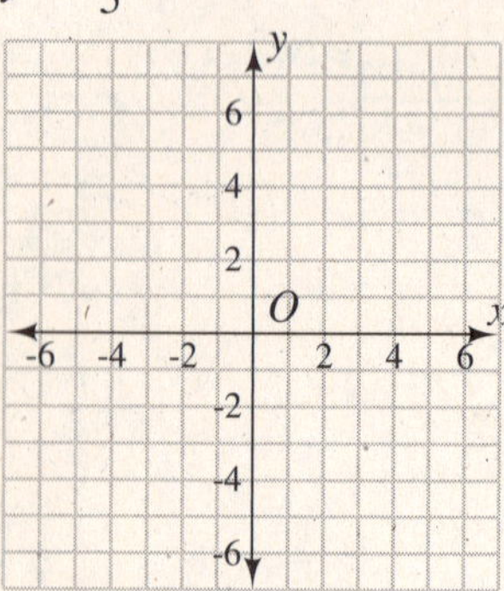

9. $y = x + 4$

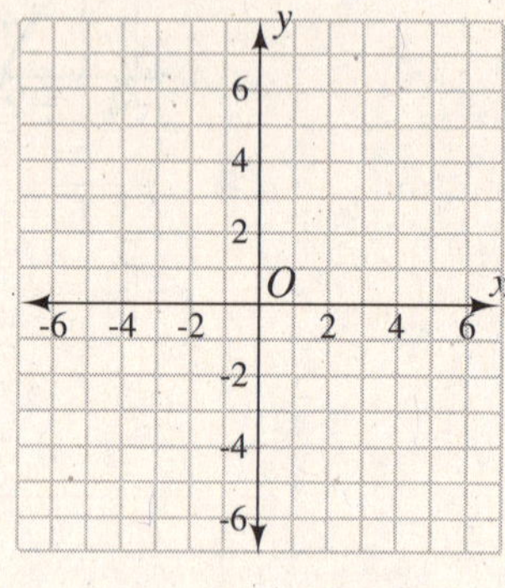

10. $y = \frac{5}{3}x - 5$

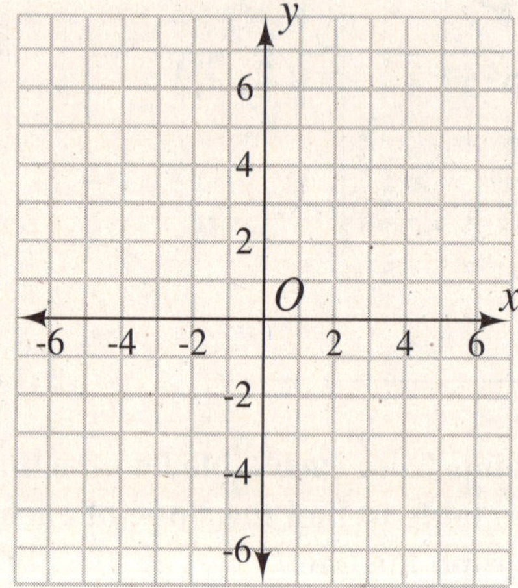

Write an equation for each line.

11.

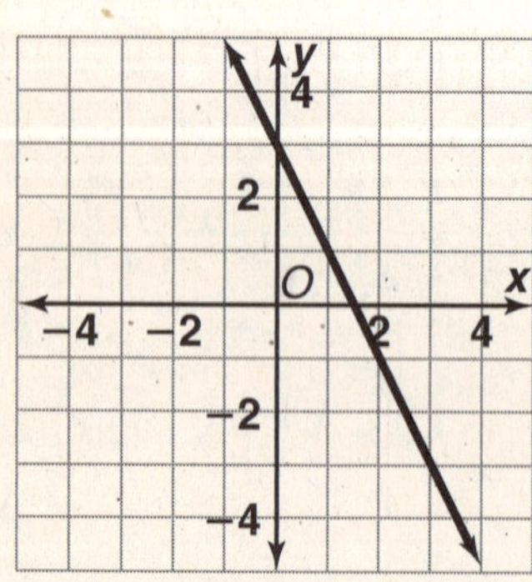

____

12.

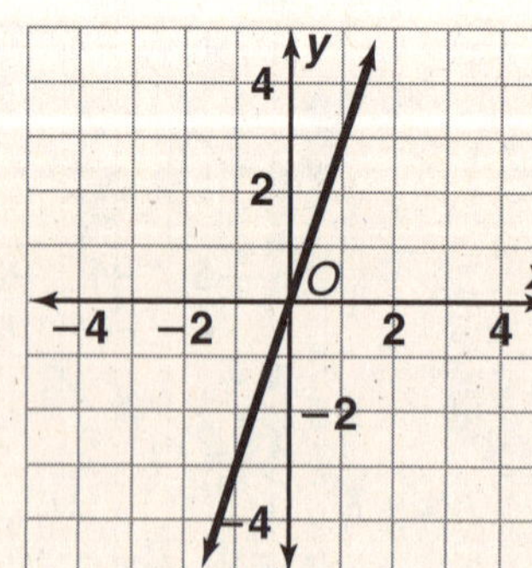

____

13.

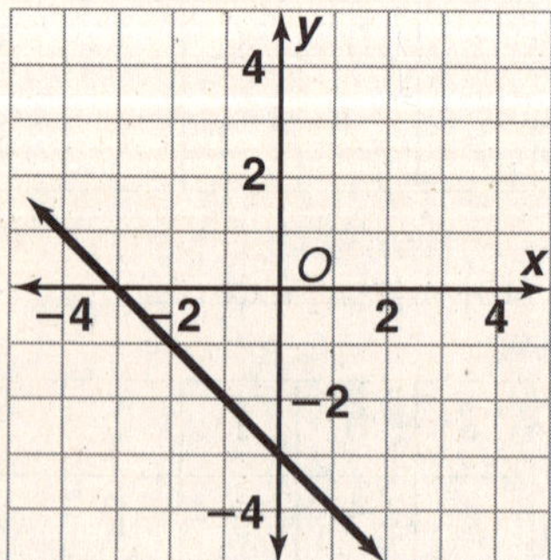

____

Practice 3-5

Problem Solving: Write an Equation and Make a Graph

Write and graph an equation with two variables to model each situation.

1. You order books through a catalog. Each book costs $12 and the shipping and handling cost is $5. Write an equation and make a graph that represents your total cost.

   ____

   a. What is the total cost if you buy 6 books? _________

   b. What is the total cost if you buy 4 books? _________

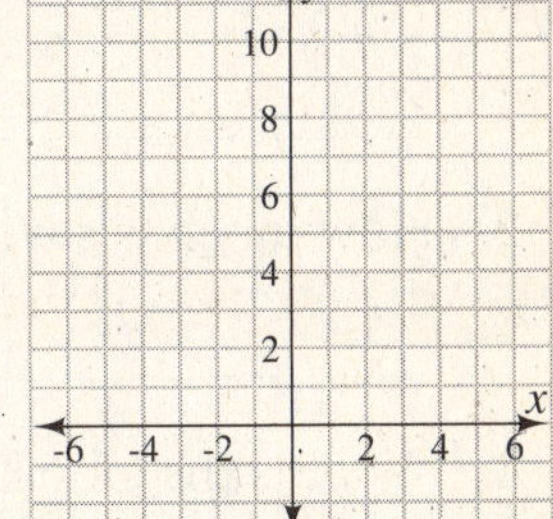

2. A ride in a taxicab costs $2.50 for the first mile and $1.50 for each additional mile, or part of a mile. Write an equation and make a graph that represents the total cost.

   ____

   a. What is the total cost of a 10-mile ride? _________

   b. What is the total cost of a 25-mile ride? _________

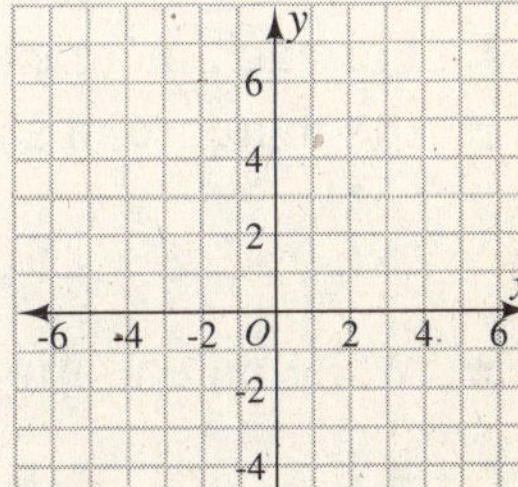
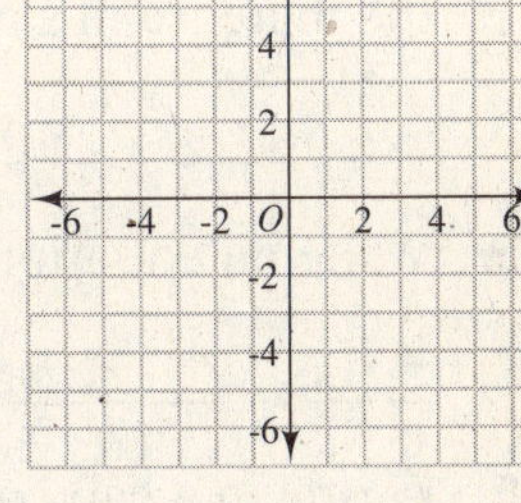
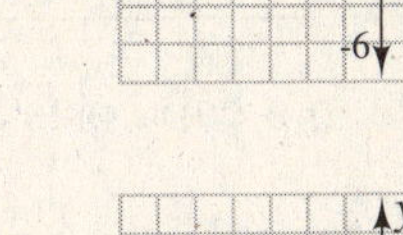

3. A tree is 3 ft tall and grows 3 in. each day. Write an equation and make a graph that represents how much the tree grows over time.

   ____

   a. How tall is the tree in a week? _________

   b. How tall is the tree in 4 weeks? _________

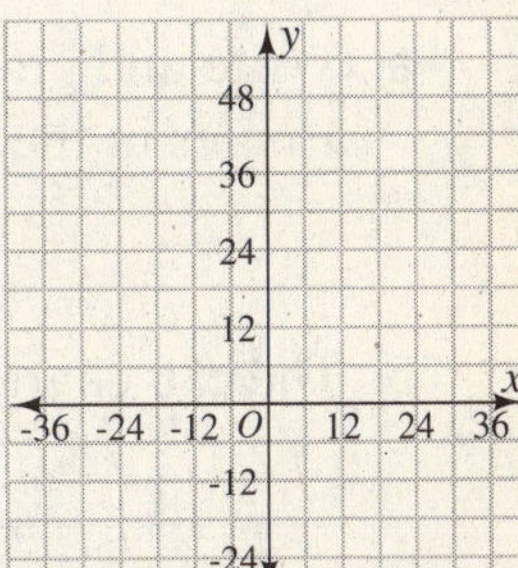

Use any strategy to solve each problem.

4. Marcy plans to save $3 in January, $4 in February, $6 in March, and $9 in April. If she continues this pattern, how much money will she save in December? _______________

5. Inez is building a fence around her square garden. She plans to put 8 posts along each side. The diameter of each post is 6 inches. How many posts will there be? _______________

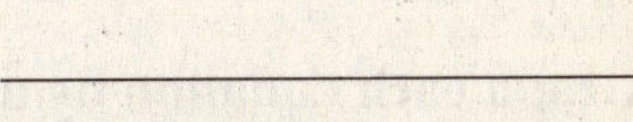
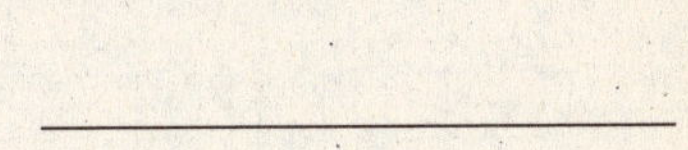

6. Alain, Betina, Coley, and Dimitri are artists. One is a potter, one a painter, one a pianist, and one a songwriter. Alain, and Coley saw the pianist perform. Betina and Coley have modeled for the painter. The writer wrote a song about Alain and Dimitri. Bettina is the potter. Who is the songwriter? _______________

7. Luis is reading a book with 520 pages. When he has read 4 times as many pages as he already has, he will be 184 pages from the end. How many pages has Luis read? _______________

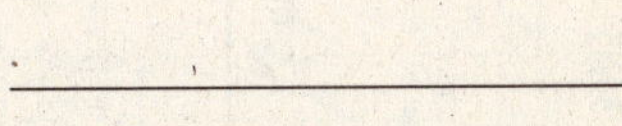

Practice 3-6

Using Graphs of Equations

Use the graph at the right for Exercises 1–5.

1. What earnings will produce $225 in savings?

   ____

2. How much is saved from earnings of $400?

   ____

3. What is the slope of the line in the graph?

   ____

4. For each increase of $200 in earnings, what is
   the increase in savings?

   ____

5. Write an equation for the line.

   ____

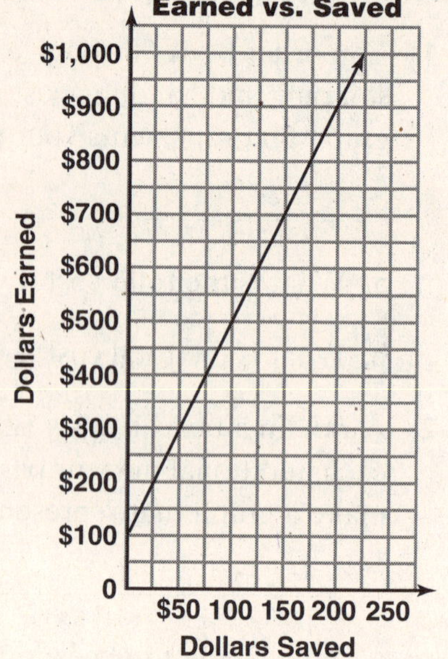

6. A ride in a cab costs $.40 plus $.15 per mile.

   a. Write and graph an equation for traveling
      x miles in the cab.

      ____

   b. The cab charges $.70 for a ride of how many miles?

      ____

   c. How much does the cab charge for a trip of 8 miles?

      ____

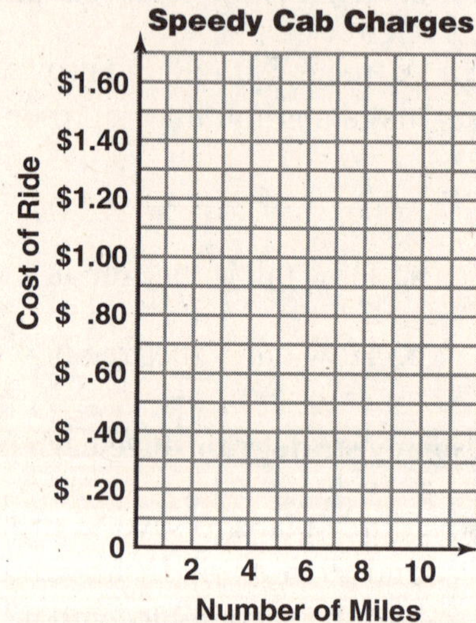

Graph each equation by using the *x*- and *y*-intercepts.

7. $2x + 3y = 6$ 8. $x - 2y = 4$ 9. $2x - y = -4$

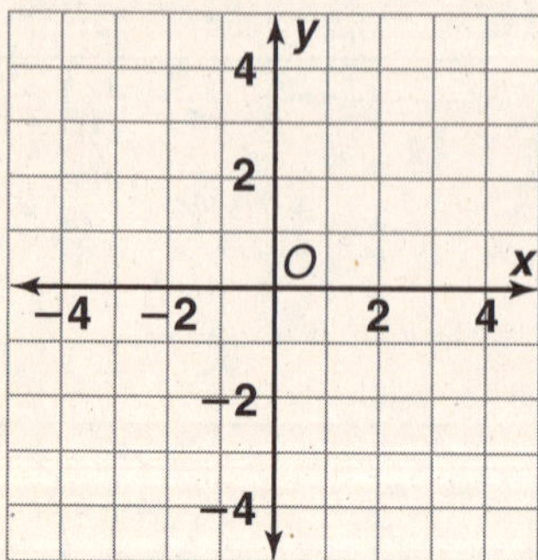
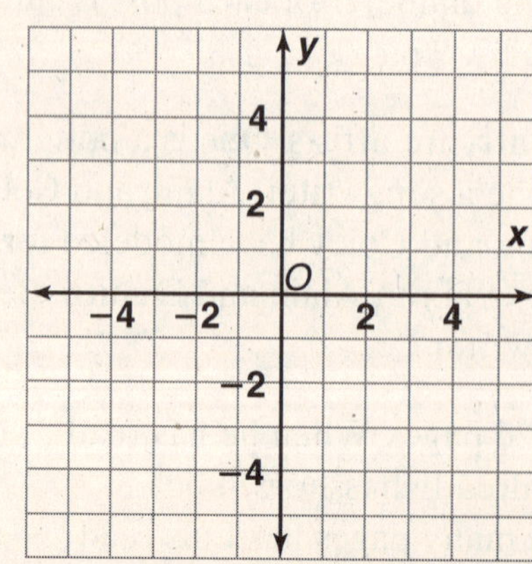
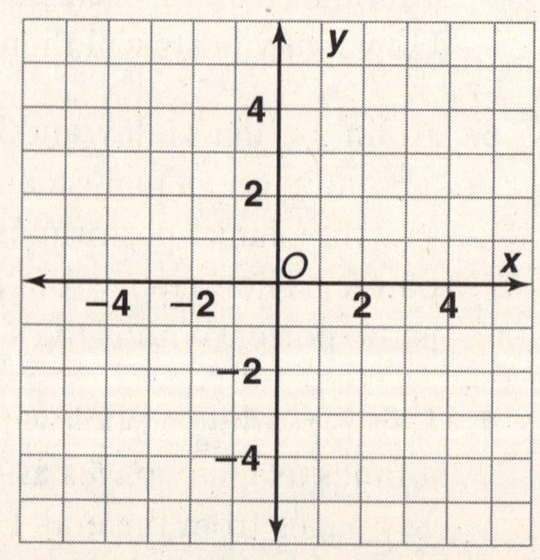

Practice 3-7

Solving Linear Systems by Graphing

Solve each system of equations by graphing.

1. $y = x + 2$
$y = 2x + 1$

Solution: _________

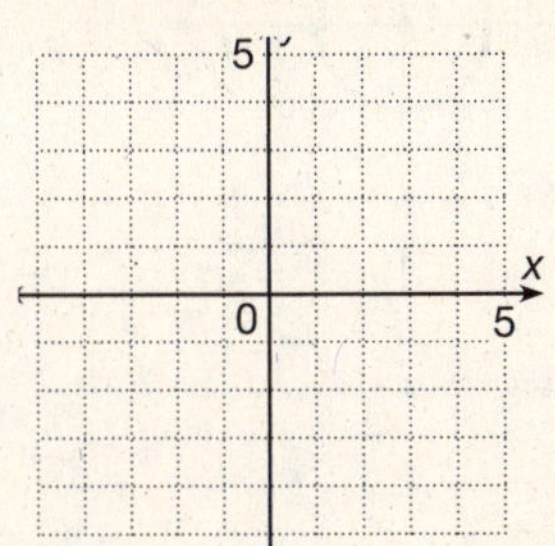

2. $y = -2x + 2$
$y = 3x + 2$

Solution: _________

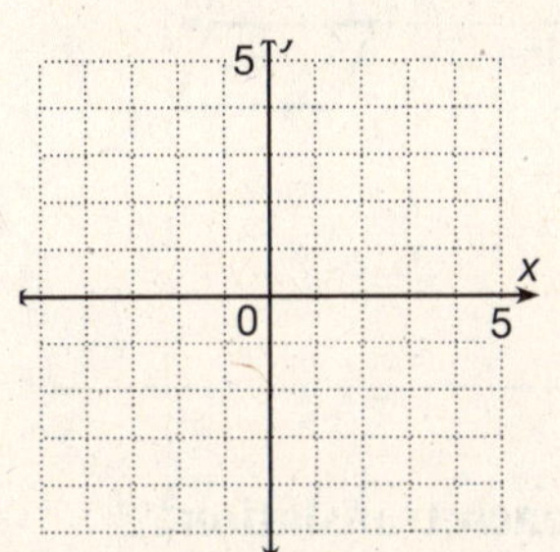

3. $y = -\frac{1}{2}x - 1$
$y = x - 4$

Solution: _________

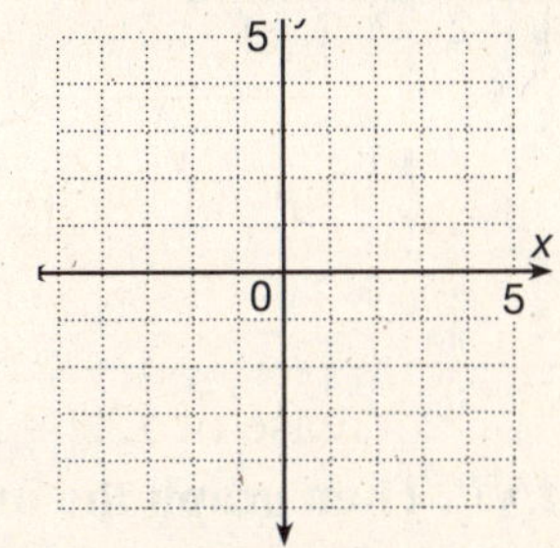

4. $y = 2x + 3$
$y = \frac{1}{2}x$

Solution: _________

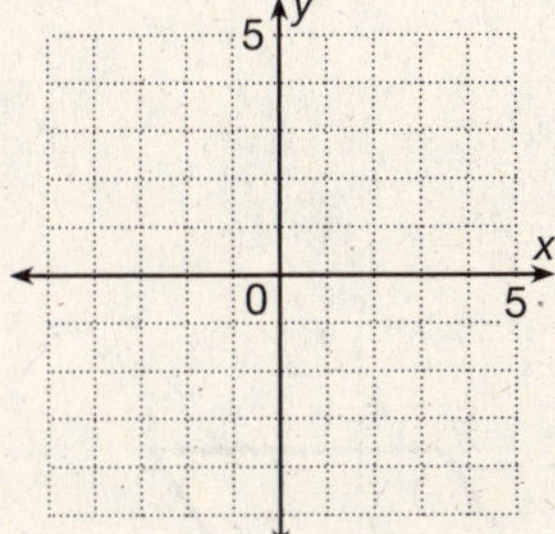

5. $y = -\frac{3}{2}x + 2$
$y = \frac{1}{2}x - 2$

Solution: _________

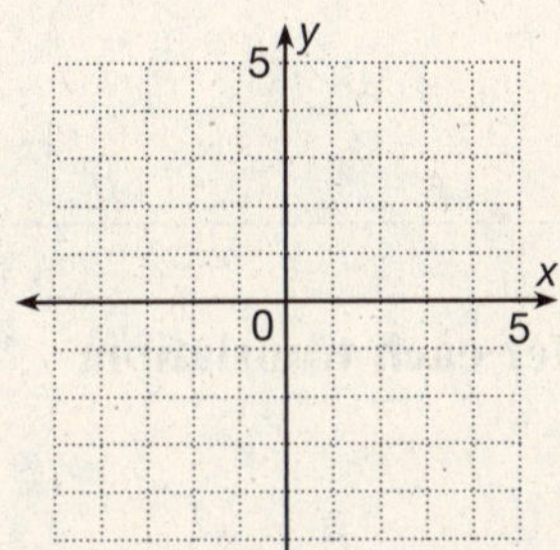

6. $y = 2x - 5$
$y = \frac{1}{4}x + 2$

Solution: _________

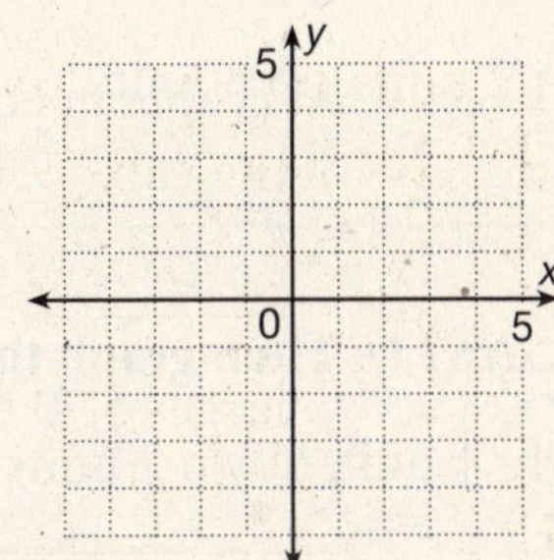

7. Tomatoes are \$.80 per pound at Rob's Market, and \$1.20 per pound at Sal's Produce. You have a coupon for \$1.40 off at Sal's. (Assume that you buy at least \$1.40 worth of tomatoes.)

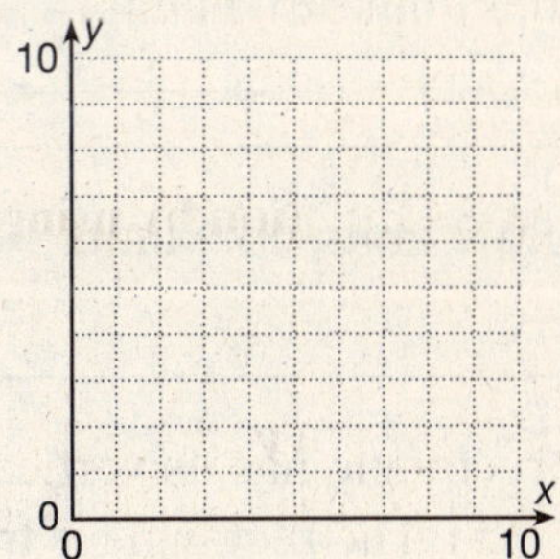

a. Write an equation relating the cost, y, to the number of pounds, x, at each market.

Rob's: _________________

Sal's: _________________

b. Use a graph to estimate the number of pounds for which the cost is the same at either store.

____

Practice 3-8

Translations

Use arrow notation to write a rule that describes the translation shown on each graph.

1.

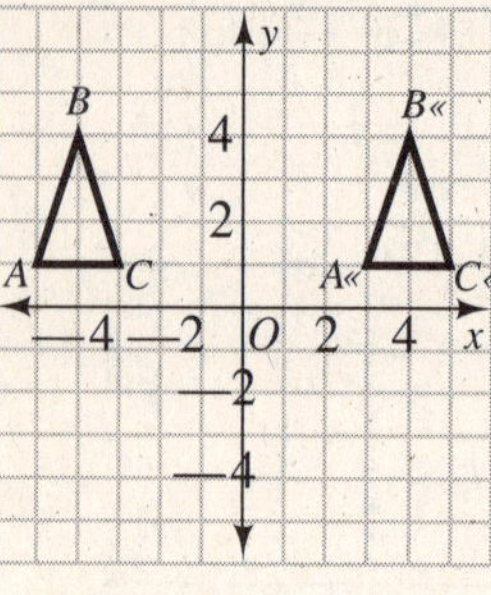

2.

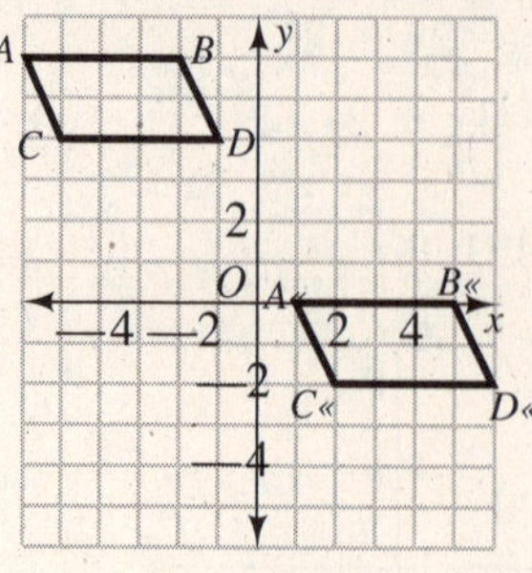

3.

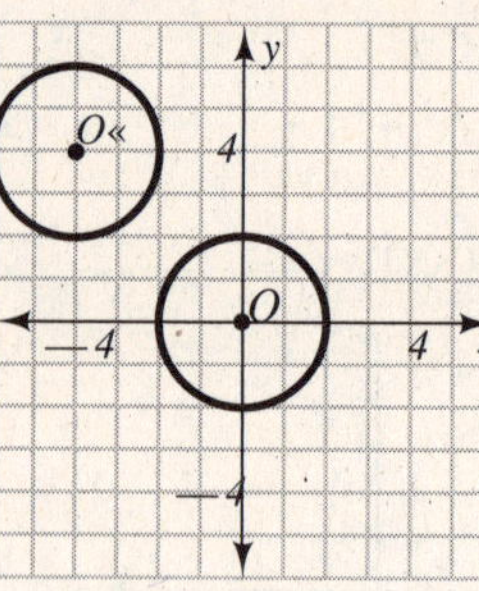

_______________   _______________   _______________

Copy △MNP. Then graph the image after each translation.

4. left 2 units, down 2 units

____

5. right 2 units, down 1 unit

____

6. left 2 units, up 3 units

____

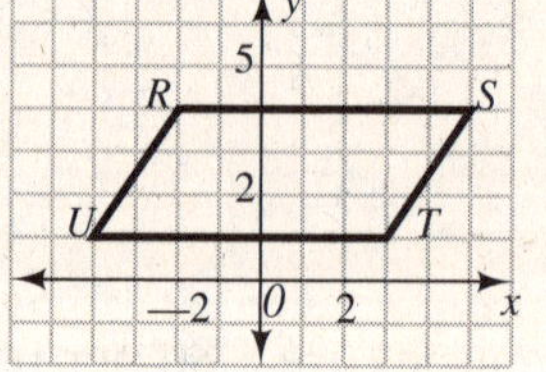

Copy ▱RSTU. Then graph the image after each translation.

7. right 1 unit, down 2 units

____

8. left 3 units, up 0 units

____

9. right 2 units, up 4 units

____

10. A rectangle has its vertices at $M(1, 1)$, $N(6, 1)$, $O(6, 5)$, and $P(1, 5)$. The rectangle is translated to the left 4 units and down 3 units. What are the coordinates of M', N', O', and P'? Graph the rectangles $MNOP$ and $M'N'O'P'$.

____

11. Use arrow notation to write a rule that describes the translation of $M'N'O'P'$ to $MNOP$.

____

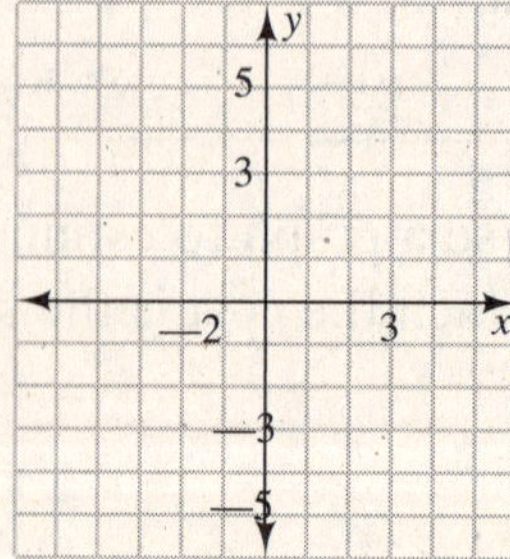

Practice 3-9

Reflections and Symmetry

How many lines of symmetry can you find for each letter?

1. W _______________ **2.** X _______________ **3.** H _______________ **4.** T _______________

Graph the given point and its image after each reflection. Name the coordinates of the reflected point.

5. $A(5, -4)$ over the vertical dashed line

6. $B(-3, 2)$ over the horizontal dashed line

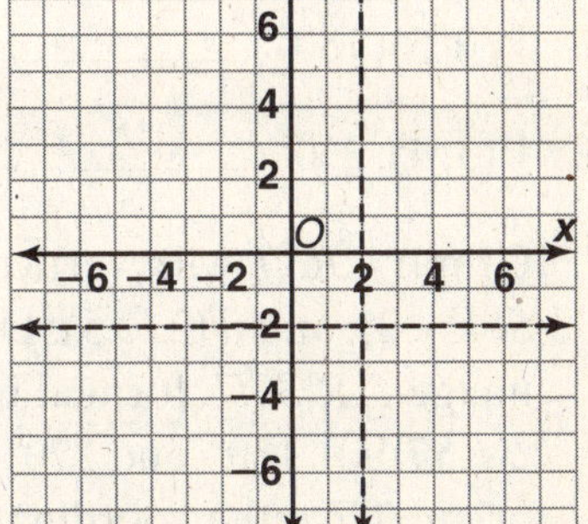

____

7. $C(-5, 0)$ over the y-axis

8. $D(3, 4)$ over the x-axis

____

$\triangle ABC$ has vertices $A(2, 1)$, $B(3, -5)$, and $C(-2, 4)$. Graph $\triangle ABC$ and its image, $\triangle A'B'C'$, after a reflection over each line. Name the coordinates of A', B', and C'.

9. the x-axis

10. the line through $(-1, 2)$ and $(1, 2)$

11. the y-axis

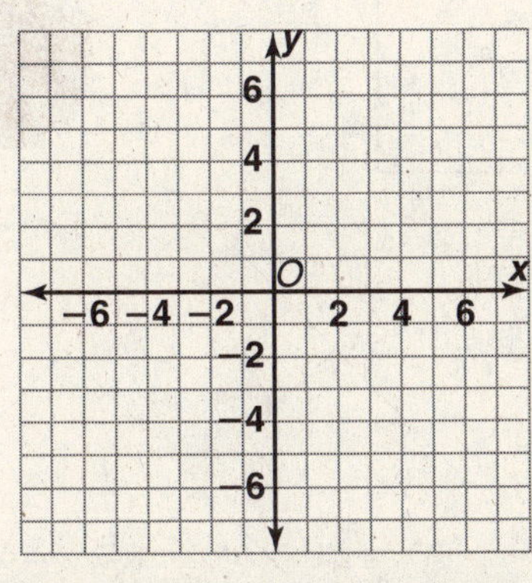

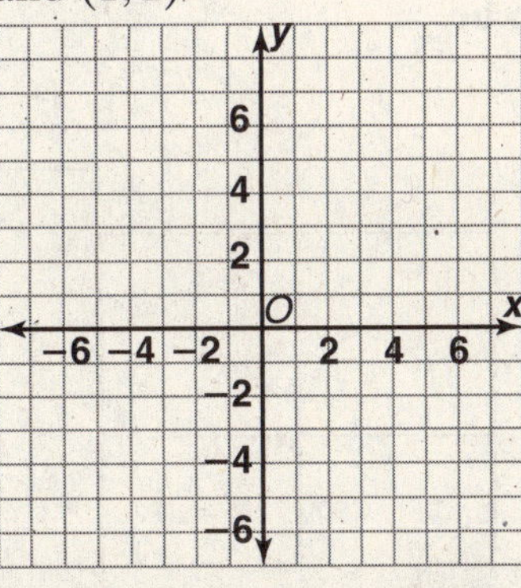

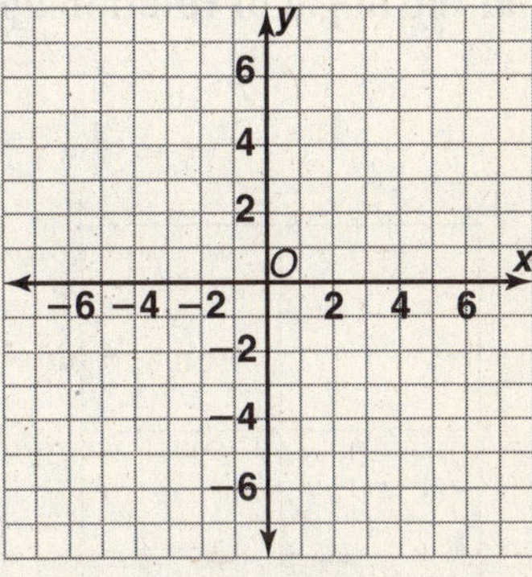

____

____

____

____

____

____

Fold your paper over each dashed line. Are the figures reflections of each other over the given line?

12. 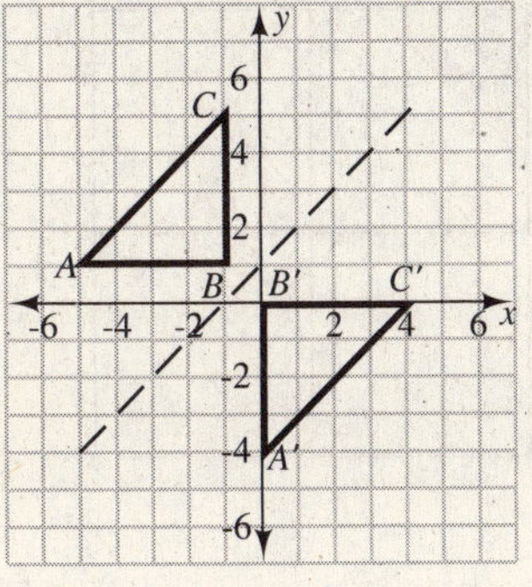

13. 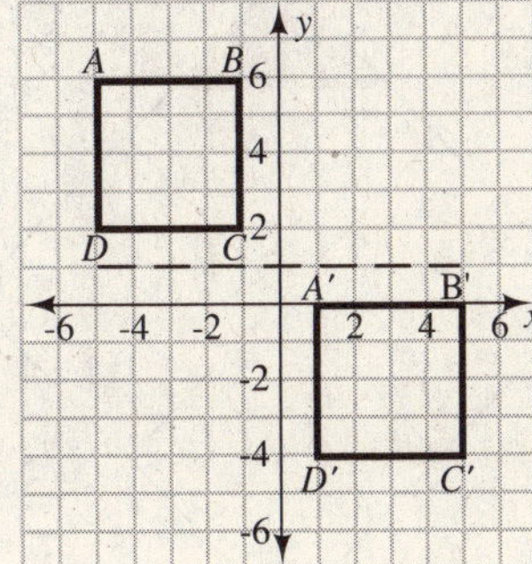

14. 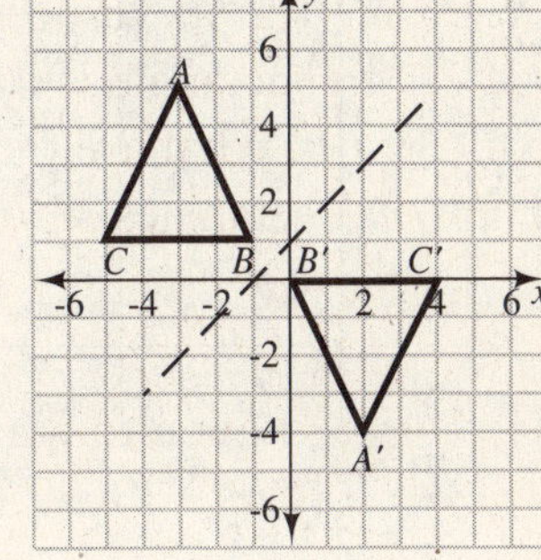

____

____

____

Practice 3-10

Rotations

Graph each point. Then rotate it the given number of degrees about the origin. Give the coordinates of the image.

1. $V(2, -3); 90°$ _______________

2. $M(-4, 5); 270°$ _______________

3. $V(0, 5); 180°$ _______________

4. $M(6, 0); 90°$ _______________

5. $V(3, 4); 360°$ _______________

6. $M(0; -1); 90°$ _______________

7. Graph $\triangle RST$ with vertices $R(-1, 3)$, $S(4, -2)$, and $T(2, -5)$. Draw the image $\triangle R'S'T'$, formed by rotating $\triangle RST$ 90°, 180°, and 270° about the origin. Give the coordinates of R', S', and T'.

90° ________________________________

180° ________________________________

270° ________________________________

Determine if each figure could be a rotation of the figure at the right. For each figure that could be a rotation, tell what the angle of rotation appears to be.

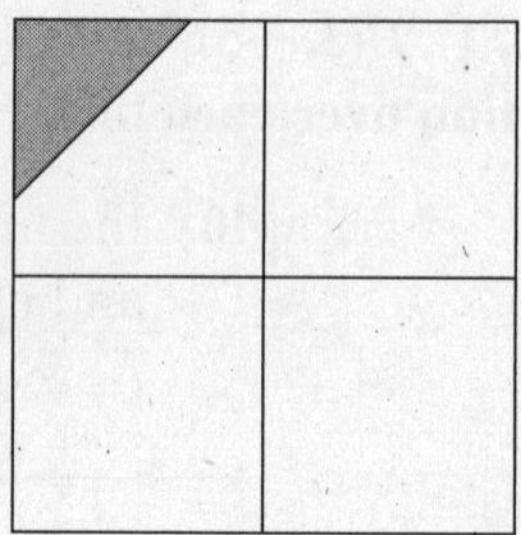

8. 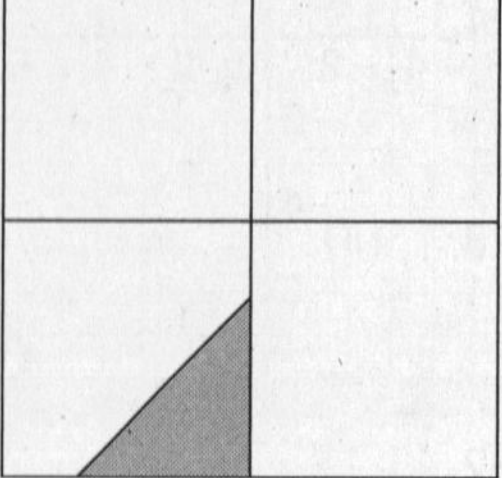

9. 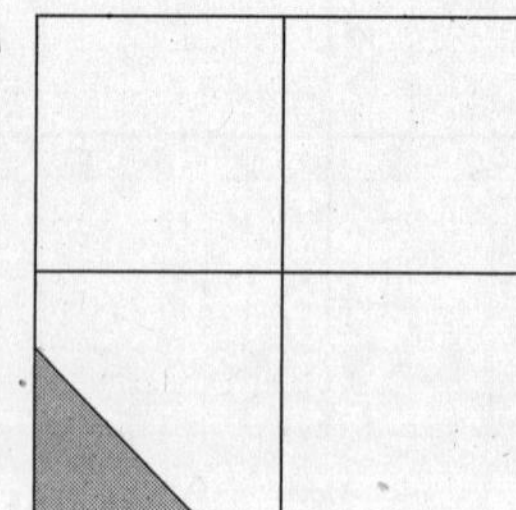

10. 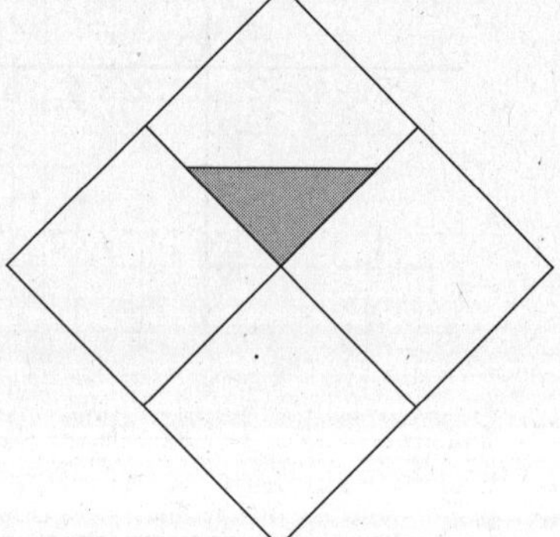

____

____

____

11. 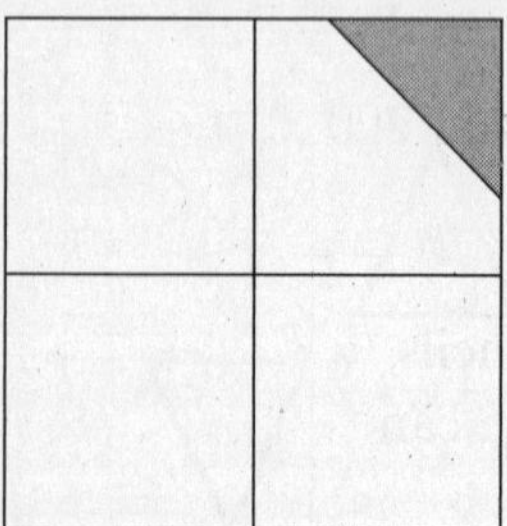

12. 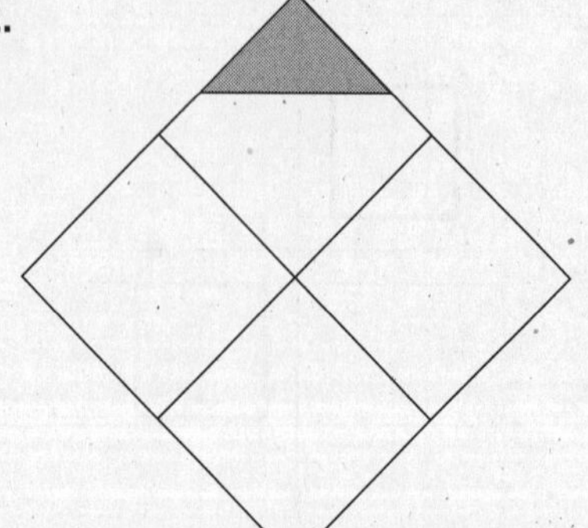

13. 

____

____

____

Practice 4-1

Factors

List all the factors of each number.

1. 36 ____________ **2.** 42 ____________ **3.** 50 ____________ **4.** 41 ____________

____________ ____________ ____________ ____________

Tell whether the first number is a factor of the second.

5. 2; 71 ________ **6.** 1; 18 ________ **7.** 3; 81 ________ **8.** 4; 74 ________

9. 9; 522 ________ **10.** 8; 508 ________ **11.** 13; 179 ________ **12.** 17; 3,587 ________

Identify each number as *prime* or *composite*. If the number is *composite*, use a factor tree to find its prime factorization.

13. 74 **14.** 83 **15.** 23 **16.** 51

________ ________ ________ ________

________ ________ ________ ________

17. 73 **18.** 91 **19.** 109 **20.** 211

________ ________ ________ ________

Write the prime factorization of each number.

21. 70 **22.** 92 **23.** 120 **24.** 118

________ ________ ________ ________

25. 200 **26.** 180 **27.** 360 **28.** 500

________ ________ ________ ________

29. 187 **30.** 364 **31.** 1,287 **32.** 1,122

________ ________ ________ ________

Find the GCF by finding the prime factorization.

33. 24, 40 **34.** 20, 42 **35.** 56, 63 **36.** 48, 72

________ ________ ________ ________

37. 18, 24, 36 **38.** 20, 45, 75 **39.** 120, 150, 180 **40.** 200, 250, 400

________ ________ ________ ________

41. Mr. Turner distributed some supplies in his office. He distributed 120 pencils, 300 paper clips, and 16 pens. What is the greatest number of people there can be in the office if each person received the same number of items? ____________

42. The baseball league bought new equipment for the teams. The managers bought 288 baseballs, 40 bats, and 24 equipment bags. How many teams are there if all the new equipment is distributed equally among the teams? ____________

Practice 4-2   **Equivalent Forms of Rational Numbers**

Write each fraction in simplest form.

1. -5 _______

2. 0.63 _______

3. -3.9 _______

4. $4\frac{5}{6}$ _______

5. $\frac{77}{99}$ _______

6. $\frac{21}{-56}$ _______

7. $-\frac{28}{52}$ _______

8. $\frac{195}{105}$ _______

9. A baseball player averaged 0.375 last season. Express the batting average as a fraction. _______

Write each fraction or mixed number as a decimal rounded to three places.

10. $\frac{7}{21}$ _______

11. $-\frac{9}{21}$ _______

12. $-\frac{2}{3}$ _______

13. $1\frac{6}{7}$ _______

14. $3\frac{1}{6}$ _______

15. $-4\frac{7}{8}$ _______

16. $3\frac{11}{12}$ _______

17. $5\frac{7}{11}$ _______

18. $-4\frac{7}{11}$ _______

19. $3\frac{1}{18}$ _______

20. $-1\frac{7}{18}$ _______

21. $2\frac{5}{12}$ _______

22. $-2\frac{7}{9}$ _______

23. $5\frac{7}{15}$ _______

24. $-4\frac{14}{15}$ _______

25. $3\frac{8}{11}$ _______

Write each decimal as a mixed number or fraction in simplest form.

26. 0.006 _______

27. $-4.\overline{8}$ _______

28. 0.97 _______

29. $0.\overline{53}$ _______

30. $0.\overline{4}$ _______

31. 9.05 _______

32. -0.28 _______

33. $5.\overline{618}$ _______

34. 3.082 _______

35. $-1.\overline{41}$ _______

36. $4.\overline{23}$ _______

37. $17.\overline{3}$ _______

38. $8.\overline{05}$ _______

39. $-3.0\overline{2}$ _______

40. $7.1\overline{3}$ _______

41. $0.\overline{2}$ _______

Solve.

42. The eighth grade held a magazine sale to raise money for their spring trip. They wanted each student to sell subscriptions. After the first day of the sale, 25 out of 125 students turned in subscription orders. Write a rational number in simplest form to express the student response on the first day.

____

43. Pete wanted to win the prize for selling the most subscriptions. Of 240 subscriptions sold, Pete sold 30. Write a rational number in simplest form to express Pete's part of the total sales.

____

Practice 4-3

Comparing and Ordering Rational Numbers

Determine which rational number is greater by rewriting each pair of fractions with the same common denominator.

1. $\frac{2}{9}, \frac{3}{6}$

2. $\frac{2}{4}, \frac{4}{5}$

3. $\frac{1}{9}, \frac{1}{3}$

4. $\frac{2}{12}, \frac{1}{4}$

5. $\frac{5}{12}, \frac{9}{15}$

6. $\frac{7}{10}, \frac{3}{5}$

7. $\frac{6}{16}, \frac{4}{9}$

8. $\frac{5}{10}, \frac{8}{12}$

9. $\frac{2}{5}, \frac{1}{3}$

10. $\frac{4}{6}, \frac{1}{3}$

11. $\frac{3}{8}, \frac{8}{9}$

12. $\frac{3}{6}, \frac{1}{3}$

13. $\frac{2}{6}, \frac{4}{5}$

14. $\frac{5}{20}, \frac{1}{2}$

15. $\frac{1}{7}, \frac{1}{10}$

16. During the 1992 Summer Olympic Games, the top three women's long jumpers were Inessa Kravets ($23\frac{3}{8}$ ft), Jackie Joyner-Kersee ($23\frac{5}{24}$ ft), and Heike Drechsler ($23\frac{7}{16}$ ft). Write these women's names in order from the shortest jump to the longest.

____

Compare. Write >, <, or =.

17. $-\frac{4}{9} \ \square \ -\frac{5}{8}$

18. $\frac{1}{3} \ \square \ \frac{6}{18}$

19. $\frac{5}{7} \ \square \ 0.63$

20. $-0.76 \ \square \ -\frac{3}{4}$

21. $-1\frac{9}{12} \ \square \ -1\frac{15}{20}$

22. $\frac{6}{11} \ \square \ \frac{5}{9}$

23. $\frac{7}{12} \ \square \ 0.59$

24. $\frac{6}{13} \ \square \ 0.45$

Order each set of numbers from greatest to least.

25. $0.74, \frac{3}{4}, \frac{6}{7}, 0.64$ _________________________

26. $\frac{16}{32}, 0.45, \frac{2}{5}, \frac{9}{25}$ _________________________

27. $\frac{7}{8}, -\frac{5}{8}, \frac{15}{30}, -\frac{8}{11}$ _________________________

28. $\frac{14}{15}, 0.743, -0.65, \frac{14}{31}$ _________________________

29. $\frac{17}{28}, 0.95, \frac{11}{15}, \frac{17}{30}$ _________________________

30. $0.8, 0.5, \frac{5}{8}, \frac{3}{8}$ _________________________

31. $\frac{7}{10}, \frac{1}{2}, -0.3, -\frac{3}{4}$ _________________________

32. $-\frac{9}{10}, -\frac{4}{5}, -\frac{1}{2}, -\frac{17}{18}$ _________________________

Practice 4-4

Adding and Subtracting Rational Numbers

Find each sum or difference as a mixed number or fraction in simplest form.

1. $\frac{3}{4} + \frac{7}{8}$ _________

2. $-1\frac{1}{6} + 2\frac{2}{3}$ _________

3. $4\frac{1}{2} - 7\frac{7}{8}$ _________

4. $-3\frac{5}{6} - \left(-4\frac{1}{12}\right)$ _________

5. $\frac{5}{18} + \frac{7}{12}$ _________

6. $-4\frac{7}{20} + 3\frac{9}{10}$ _________

7. $5\frac{8}{21} - \left(-3\frac{1}{7}\right)$ _________

8. $1\frac{19}{24} + 2\frac{23}{20}$ _________

9. $3\frac{16}{25} - 4\frac{7}{20}$ _________

10. $5\frac{1}{14} + 2\frac{3}{7} + 1\frac{4}{21}$ _________

11. $\frac{11}{12} - \frac{5}{16} + \frac{11}{18}$ _________

12. $\frac{5}{6} + \frac{7}{8} - \frac{11}{12}$ _________

13. $-19\frac{5}{6} + 10\frac{9}{10}$ _________

14. $4\frac{7}{18} - 3\frac{7}{12}$ _________

15. $-1\frac{4}{5} - \left(-4\frac{1}{12}\right)$ _________

Write each answer as a fraction or mixed number in simplest form.

16. $14.6 + \left(-3\frac{1}{5}\right)$

17. $-7\frac{3}{4} - 4.125$

18. $5.75 + \left(-2\frac{1}{8}\right)$

____

____

____

19. $1\frac{3}{4} - 2.75 - 4\frac{5}{8}$

20. $3\frac{1}{2} - 6\frac{7}{10} + 4\frac{1}{5}$

21. $\frac{3}{16} + \frac{1}{8} - \frac{1}{4}$

____

____

____

Solve each equation. Write each answer as a mixed number or as a fraction in simplest form.

22. $x + \frac{3}{8} = -\frac{1}{4}$

23. $y - \frac{1}{5} = -\frac{4}{5}$

24. $z + \left(-\frac{2}{3}\right) = -\frac{1}{6}$

____

____

____

25. $m - \frac{9}{10} = \frac{1}{5}$

26. $n - 1\frac{1}{3} = -3$

27. $p + \frac{7}{12} = -\frac{1}{4}$

____

____

____

28. $c - 7.2 = -3.7$

29. $d - 0.16 = 2.3$

30. $\frac{1}{8} + a = -2\frac{1}{4}$

____

____

____

31. Stanley is helping in the library by mending torn pages. He has cut strips of tape with lengths of $5\frac{1}{2}$ in., $6\frac{7}{8}$ in., $3\frac{3}{4}$ in., and $4\frac{3}{16}$ in. What is the total length of tape he has used?

____

Practice 4-5

Multiplying and Dividing Rational Numbers

Find each product or quotient. Write each answer as a fraction or mixed number in simplest form.

1. $-\frac{1}{6} \cdot 2\frac{3}{4}$ _________

2. $\frac{3}{16} \div \left(-\frac{1}{8}\right)$ _________

3. $-\frac{31}{56} \cdot (-8)$ _________

4. $-5\frac{7}{12} \div 12$ _________

5. $-8 \div \frac{1}{4}$ _________

6. $-3\frac{1}{6} \div \left(-2\frac{1}{12}\right)$ _________

7. $8\frac{3}{4} \cdot 3\frac{7}{8}$ _________

8. $-\frac{11}{12} \div \frac{5}{6}$ _________

9. $4\frac{9}{28} \cdot (-7)$ _________

10. $-1\frac{1}{15} \div 15$ _________

11. $-3 \div \frac{3}{4}$ _________

12. $-2\frac{7}{8} \div 3\frac{3}{4}$ _________

13. $-\frac{23}{24} \cdot (-8)$ _________

14. $\frac{7}{8} \cdot \left(-\frac{2}{7}\right)$ _________

15. $-7 \div \frac{1}{9}$ _________

16. $-6\frac{5}{6} \div \frac{1}{6}$ _________

17. $-8 \cdot 3\frac{3}{4}$ _________

18. $\frac{7}{10} \cdot \left(-3\frac{1}{4}\right)$ _________

19. $5 \cdot \left(-3\frac{5}{6}\right)$ _________

20. $-\frac{8}{9} \div \left(-3\frac{2}{3}\right)$ _________

21. $2\frac{1}{3} \div \frac{2}{3}$ _________

Solve each equation.

22. $\frac{1}{3}a = \frac{3}{10}$

23. $-\frac{3}{4}b = 9$

24. $-\frac{7}{8}c = 4\frac{2}{3}$

____

25. $\frac{5}{6}n = -3\frac{3}{4}$

26. $-\frac{3}{5}x = 12$

27. $-2\frac{2}{3}y = 3\frac{1}{3}$

____

28. $\frac{7}{12}y = -2\frac{4}{5}$

29. $2\frac{1}{4}z = -\frac{1}{9}$

30. $2\frac{1}{5}d = -\frac{1}{2}$

____

31. One pound of flour contains about four cups. A recipe calls for $2\frac{1}{4}$ c of flour. How many full recipes can you make from a two-pound bag of flour?

32. Kim needs $2\frac{1}{2}$ ft of wrapping paper to wrap each package. She has five packages to wrap. How many packages can she wrap with a 12-ft roll of wrapping paper?

33. Gina and Paul are making pizza for the cast and crew of the school play. They estimate that the boys in the cast and crew will eat $\frac{1}{2}$ pizza each. They estimate that the girls will each eat $\frac{1}{3}$ of a pizza. There are 7 boys and 10 girls working on the play. How many pizzas do they need to make?

Practice 4-6   **Formulas**

Find the area and the perimeter of each figure.

1. 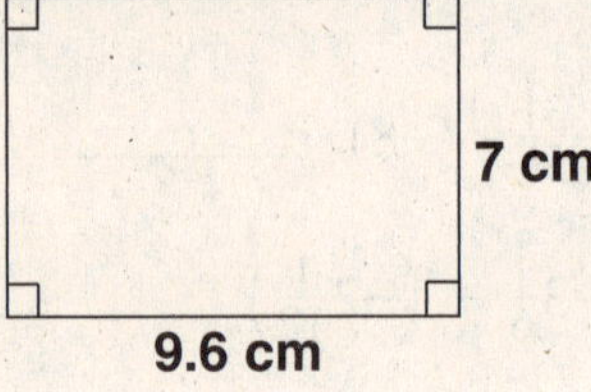

____

2. 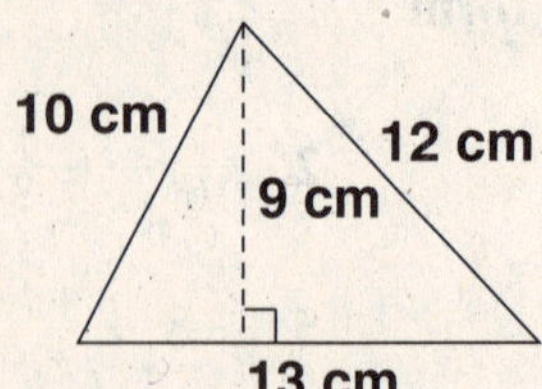

____

3. 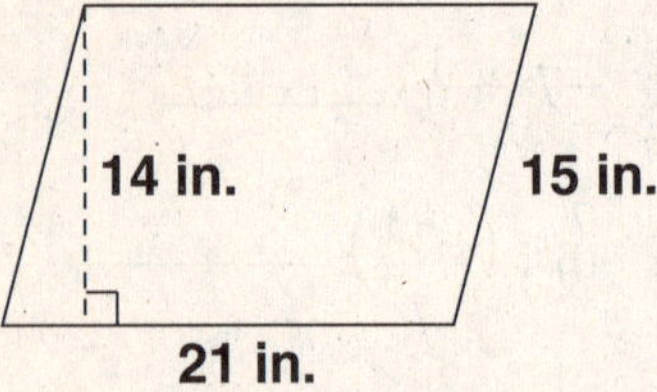

____

4. 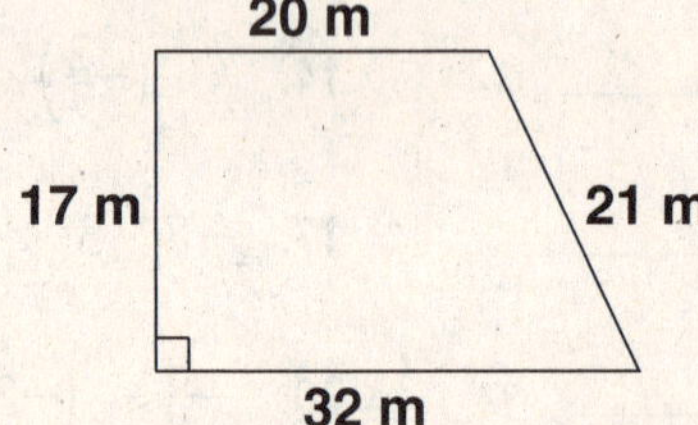

____

Write an equation to find the the solution for each problem. Solve the equation. Then give the solution for the problem.

5. The Kents left home at 7:00 A.M. and drove to their parents' house 400 mi away. They arrived at 3:00 P.M. What was their average speed?

____

6. An airplane flew for 4 h 30 min at an average speed of 515 mi/h. How far did it fly?

____

7. Marcia rowed her boat 18 mi downstream at a rate of 12 mi/h. How long did the trip take?

____

In Exercises 8–11, use the formula $F = \frac{9}{5}C + 32$ or $C = \frac{5}{9}(F - 32)$ to find a temperature in either degrees Fahrenheit, °F, or degrees Celsius, °C.

8. What is the temperature in degrees Fahrenheit when it is 0°C?

____

9. What is the temperature in degrees Fahrenheit when it is 100°C?

____

10. What is the temperature in degrees Celsius when it is −4°F?

____

11. What is the temperature in degrees Celsius when it is 77°F?

____

Practice 4-7
Problem Solving: Try, Check, and Revise and Work Backward

Solve each problem by either testing and revising or working backward.

1. Alli withdrew some money from the bank for shopping. She spent two thirds of what she withdrew on groceries. She spent $25 on a sweater. She spent half of what remained on a necklace. She went home with $15. How much did Alli withdraw from the bank?

   ____

2. Jill met her friends at the movies at 2 P.M. on Saturday after washing windows. It took her $\frac{3}{4}$ h to wash the windows at the first house. It took twice as long to wash the windows at the next house. The last house took $1\frac{1}{2}$ h. After that, it took her $\frac{1}{2}$ h to walk to the movie theater. At what time did Jill start washing windows?

   ____

3. If you start with a number, add 4, multiply by 3, subtract 10, then divide by 4, the result is 5. What is the number?

   ____

4. Phil had a busy day with his tow truck. He did not return to the garage until 4:00 P.M. It took $1\frac{3}{4}$ h to get the car back to the garage from the last call. The call before that took Phil twice as long. He took a half hour for lunch. One call in the morning took Phil only a half hour, but the one before that took five times as long. What time did Phil's work day begin?

   ____

5. A ball is bouncing on the floor. After each bounce, the height of the ball is one-half its previous height. After the fifth bounce, the height of the ball is 6 in. What was the height of the ball before the first bounce?

   ____

6. If you start with a number, subtract 4, multiply by $\frac{1}{4}$, add 6, then divide by 2, the result is 10. What is the number?

   ____

7. Matt spent $\frac{1}{5}$ of his money on a concert ticket. He spent $60 on a new jacket and $2.50 for bus fare. He reached home with $17.50. How much did he have to begin with?

   ____

8. Bob sells planters at craft shows. At the first craft show, he sold a fourth of his planters. At the next craft show, he sold 14 more. At the third he sold half of what remained. At the fourth show he sold the remaining 20. How many planters did Bob sell?

   ____

Practice 4-8

Exploring Square Roots and Irrational Numbers

Find each square root. Round to the nearest tenth if necessary.

1. $\sqrt{81}$ **2.** $\sqrt{76}$ **3.** $\sqrt{121}$ **4.** $\sqrt{289}$

5. $\sqrt{130}$ **6.** $\sqrt{8}$ **7.** $\sqrt{144}$ **8.** $\sqrt{160}$

9. $\sqrt{182}$ **10.** $\sqrt{256}$ **11.** $\sqrt{301}$ **12.** $\sqrt{350}$

13. $\sqrt{361}$ **14.** $\sqrt{410}$ **15.** $\sqrt{441}$ **16.** $\sqrt{500}$

Identify each number as rational or irrational.

17. $\sqrt{16}$ **18.** $\sqrt{11}$ **19.** $\sqrt{196}$

20. $\sqrt{200}$ **21.** $\sqrt{1,521}$ **22.** $\sqrt{785}$

23. $\sqrt{529}$ **24.** $\sqrt{1,680}$ **25.** $\sqrt{2,000}$

26. $\sqrt{3,969}$ **27.** $\sqrt{3,192}$ **28.** $\sqrt{15,376}$

29. $\frac{4}{5}$ **30.** $0.\overline{712}$ **31.** -8

32. $\sqrt{3}$ **33.** 5.2 **34.** 52

35. $-\sqrt{25}$ **36.** $\sqrt{306}$ **37.** 2.7064

Find each square root. Where necessary, round to the nearest tenth.

38. $\sqrt{5}$ **39.** $\sqrt{4}$ **40.** $\sqrt{3}$

41. $\sqrt{245}$ **42.** $\sqrt{21}$ **43.** $\sqrt{50}$

Practice 4-9

The Pythagorean Theorem

Find the missing length. If necessary, round the answer to the nearest tenth.

1.
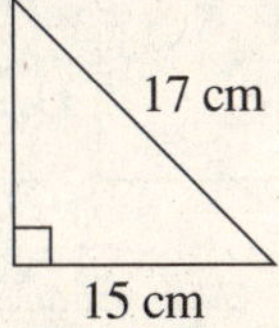

____

2.
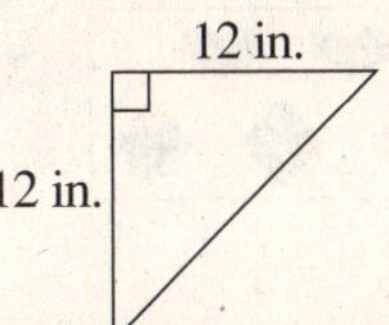

____

3.
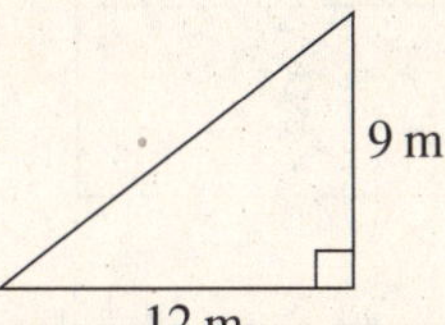

____

4.
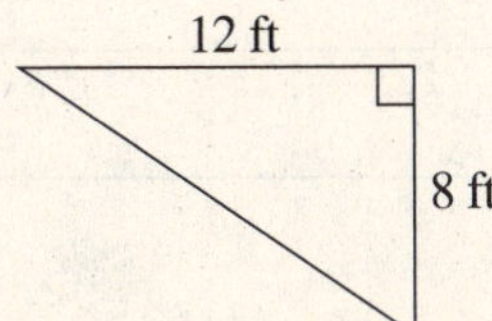

____

5.
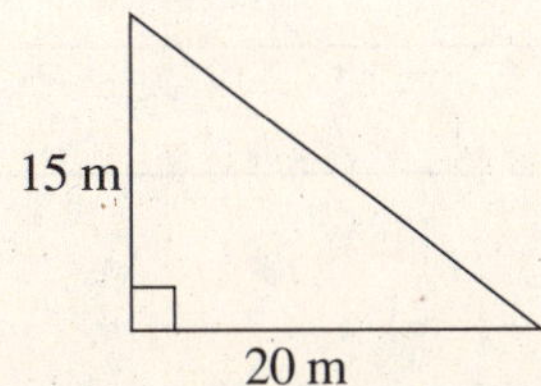

____

6.
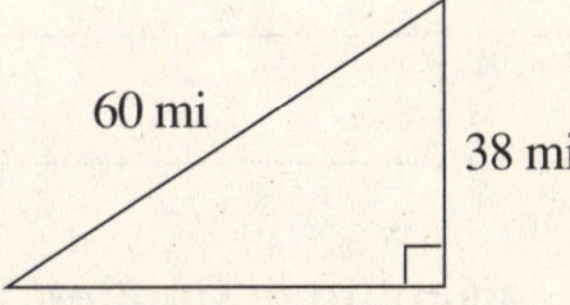

____

Is a triangle with the given side lengths a right triangle?

7. 8 cm, 12 cm, 15 cm

____

8. 9 in., 12 in., 15 in.

____

9. 5 m, 12 m, 25 m

____

10. 15 in., 36 in., 39 in.

____

11. 10 m, 20 m, 25 m

____

12. 7 mm, 24 mm, 25 mm

____

13. 9 yd, 40 yd, 41 yd

____

14. 10 cm, 25 cm, 26 cm

____

15. 27 yd, 120 yd, 130 yd

____

16. 11 mi, 60 mi, 61 mi

____

You are given three circles, as shown. Points *A, B, C, D, E, F,* and *G* lie on the same line. Find each length to the nearest tenth.

17. *HD* _______________   **18.** *IE* _______________   **19.** *JD* _______________

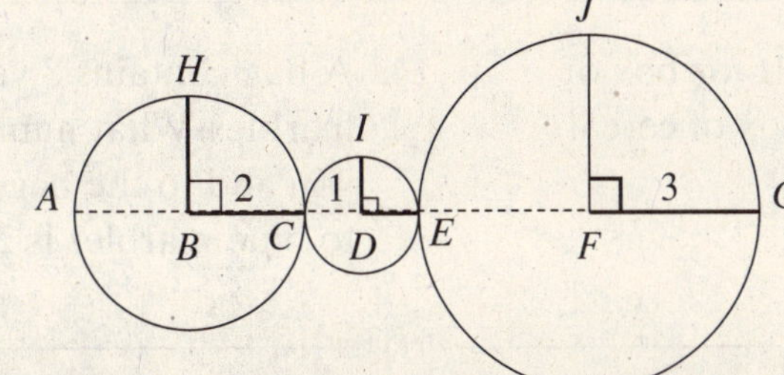

Practice 5-1 **Ratios and Rates**

Write three ratios that each diagram can represent.

1. 

____

____

____

____

2. 

____

____

____

____

3. 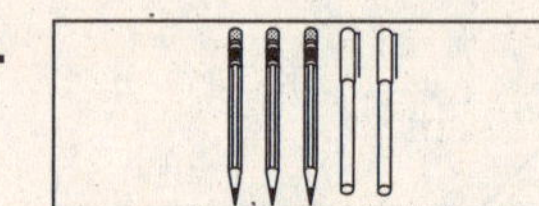

____

____

____

____

Write each ratio in simplest form.

4. 9 cm : 12 cm

5. 20 in. out of 25 in.

6. 16 ft to 24 ft

7. $\dfrac{6 \text{ m}}{21 \text{ m}}$

8. 100 yd to 85 yd

9. $\dfrac{18 \text{ km}}{30 \text{ km}}$

10. 6 in. to 2 ft

11. 10 min to 3 h

12. 20 s to 5 min

Use a calculator, paper and pencil, or mental math to find each unit rate.

13. $67.92 for 4 gal

14. $21.00 for 6 h

15. 250 mi in 4 h

16. 141 words in 3 min

17. $5.94 for 6 carnations

18. 36 min for 12 songs

The table at the right shows the results of a survey. Write each of the ratios in simplest form and as a decimal to the nearest hundredth.

Which Meal Do You Want for the Party?	
Tacos	Pizza
⌿⌿⌿⌿ ⌿⌿⌿⌿ ⌿⌿⌿⌿	⌿⌿⌿⌿ ⌿⌿⌿⌿ ⌿⌿⌿⌿ ⌿⌿⌿⌿ ⌿

19. *Tacos* to *Pizza* _______________

20. *Pizza* to *Tacos* _______________

21. *Tacos* to the total _______________

22. *Pizza* to the total _______________

23. Which is the better buy: a 16-oz box of cereal for $3.89 or a 6-oz box of cereal for $1.55?

24. A bag contains 8 yellow marbles and 6 blue marbles. What number of yellow marbles can you add to the bag so that the ratio of yellow to blue marbles is 2 : 1?

Practice 5-2

Choosing and Converting Units

Choose an appropriate customary unit.

1. length of a stapler

____

2. weight of a cookie

____

3. capacity of a teakettle

____

4. height of a door

____

5. distance to the moon

____

6. weight of a jet aircraft

____

Choose an appropriate metric unit.

7. mass of a cat

____

8. length of a playground

____

9. capacity of a test tube

____

10. length of an insect

____

11. capacity of a bathtub

____

12. mass of a coin

____

Use dimensional analysis to convert each measure. Round answers to the nearest hundredth where necessary.

13. 56 in. = _?_ ft

____

14. 240 d = _?_ h

____

15. 4 gal = _?_ pt

____

16. 0.75 d = _?_ h

____

17. 2.25 t = _?_ lb

____

18. 84 ft = _?_ yd

____

19. 0.25 d = _?_ min

____

20. 18 d = _?_ h

____

21. 0.01 t = _?_ oz

____

Use dimensional analysis to solve each problem.

22. At one time, trains were not permitted to go faster than 12 mi/h. How many yards per minute is this?

____

23. A mosquito can fly at 0.6 mi/h. How many inches per second is this?

____

24. An Arctic tern flew 11,000 miles in 115 days. How many feet per minute did the bird average?

____

25. A sneeze can travel up to 100 mi/h. How many feet per second is this?

____

Use compatible numbers to find a reasonable estimate.

26. 118 in. is about _?_ ft.

____

27. 3,540 seconds is about _?_ hours.

____

Practice 5-3

Problem Solving: Write an Equation

Solve each problem by writing an equation.

1. The P.E. department has a set of 40 jump ropes. There are 4 times more red jump ropes than blue jump ropes. How many of each color are there?

   ____

2. A snack is made from granola and nuts. In a 28-oz container, there is 1 more ounce of granola than twice the ounces of nuts. How many ounces of each are in the snack?

   ____

3. The local fair sells tickets for both children and adults. The price of a child's ticket is $5 and the price of an adult ticket is $8. The fair had its greatest turn out so far on Friday; 1,050 people attended. The fair took in $7,350. How many of each type of ticket were sold?

   ____

4. A bathroom cleaner contains 1 part of bleach with 4 parts of water. If you need 10 parts of bathroom cleaner, how much water and bleach do you need?

   ____

5. Your teacher has a container of yellow and green marbles on her desk. Your teacher says there are 3 times more green marbles than yellow marbles and there are 164 marbles in all. How many of each is in the container?

   ____

Use any strategy to solve each problem. Show your work.

6. Of 24 students questioned, 6 belong to the Music Club, 8 belong to the Math Club, 5 belong to both. How many students belong to neither club?

   ____

7. You want to carpet a room that is 9 ft long and 4 yd wide. Carpet costs $8.95 per square yard. How much carpet do you need?

   ____

8. Suppose you bought some 32¢ stamps and some 20¢ stamps. You spent $3.92 for sixteen stamps. How many of each stamp did you buy?

   ____

Practice 5-4

Solving Proportions

Solve each proportion.

1. $\frac{3}{8} = \frac{m}{16}$ _______

2. $\frac{9}{4} = \frac{27}{x}$ _______

3. $\frac{18}{6} = \frac{j}{1}$ _______

4. $\frac{b}{18} = \frac{7}{6}$ _______

5. $\frac{12}{q} = \frac{3}{4}$ _______

6. $\frac{3}{2} = \frac{15}{r}$ _______

7. $\frac{5}{x} = \frac{25}{15}$ _______

8. $\frac{80}{20} = \frac{4}{n}$ _______

Estimate the solution of each proportion.

9. $\frac{m}{25} = \frac{16}{98}$ _______

10. $\frac{7}{3} = \frac{52}{n}$ _______

11. $\frac{30}{5.9} = \frac{k}{10}$ _______

12. $\frac{2.8}{j} = \frac{1.3}{2.71}$ _______

13. $\frac{y}{12} = \frac{2.89}{4.23}$ _______

14. $\frac{5}{8} = \frac{b}{63}$ _______

15. $\frac{9}{4} = \frac{35}{d}$ _______

16. $\frac{c}{7} = \frac{28}{50}$ _______

Solve each proportion.

17. $\frac{4}{5} = \frac{b}{40}$

18. $\frac{11}{7} = \frac{88}{c}$

19. $\frac{x}{1.4} = \frac{28}{5.6}$

20. $\frac{0.99}{a} = \frac{9}{11}$

21. $\frac{42.5}{20} = \frac{x}{8}$

22. $\frac{15}{25} = \frac{7.5}{y}$

23. $\frac{16}{b} = \frac{56}{38.5}$

24. $\frac{z}{54} = \frac{5}{12}$

25. $\frac{8}{12} = \frac{e}{3}$

26. $\frac{v}{35} = \frac{15}{14}$

27. $\frac{60}{n} = \frac{12}{5}$

28. $\frac{6}{16} = \frac{9}{w}$

29. $\frac{4}{7} = \frac{r}{35}$

30. $\frac{18}{16} = \frac{27}{t}$

31. $\frac{n}{12} = \frac{12.5}{15}$

32. $\frac{27}{f} = \frac{40.5}{31.5}$

33. 5 is to 8 as 15 is to w

34. y is to 8 as 22.5 is to 10

35. 14 is to b as 28 is to 18

36. 10 is to 7 as m is to 10.5

37. 30 is to 16 as j is to 8

38. r is to 17 as 81 is to 51

Write a proportion for each situation. Then solve.

39. Jaime paid $1.29 for three ponytail holders. At that rate, what would eight ponytail holders cost her?

40. According to a label, there are 25 calories per serving of turkey lunch meat. How many calories are there in 2.5 servings?

41. Arturo paid $8 in tax on a purchase of $200. At that rate, what would the tax be on a purchase of $150?

42. Chris drove 200 mi in 4 h. At that rate, how long would it take Chris to drive 340 mi?

Practice 5-5

Similar Figures and Proportions

Tell whether each pair of polygons is similar. Explain why or why not.

1. 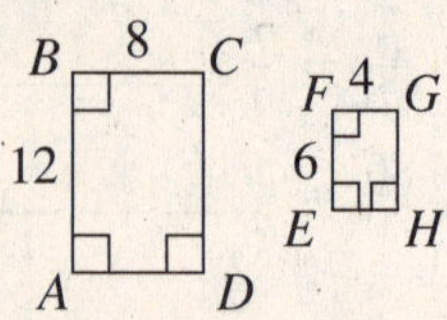

2. 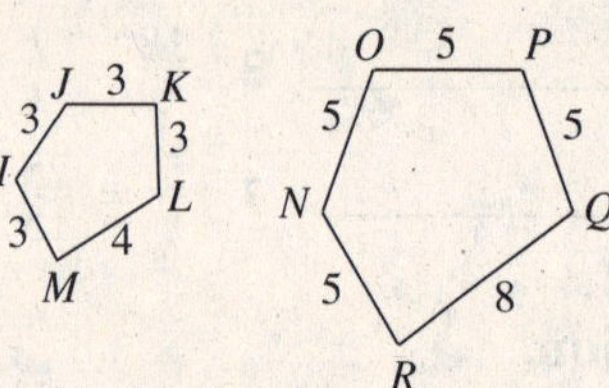

3. 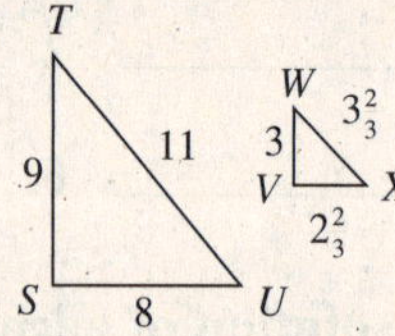

____

____

____

4. 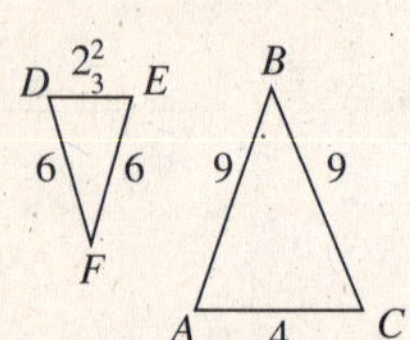

5. 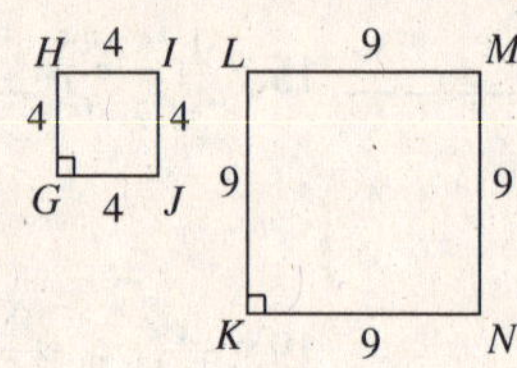

6. 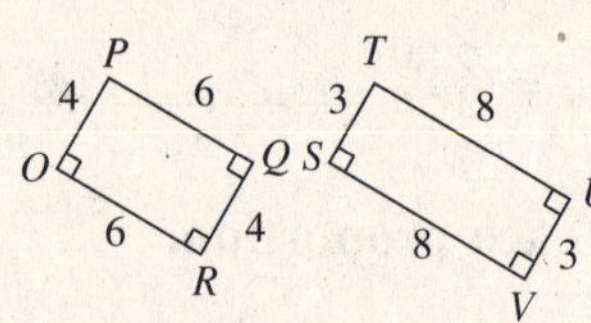

____

____

____

Exercise 7–14 show pairs of similar polygons. Find the unknown lengths.

7. 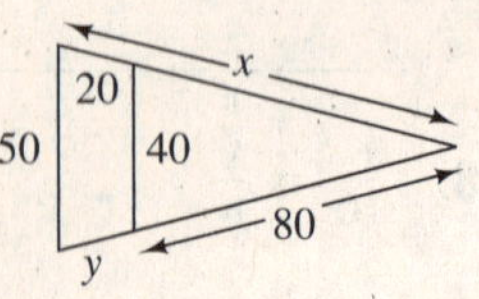

8. 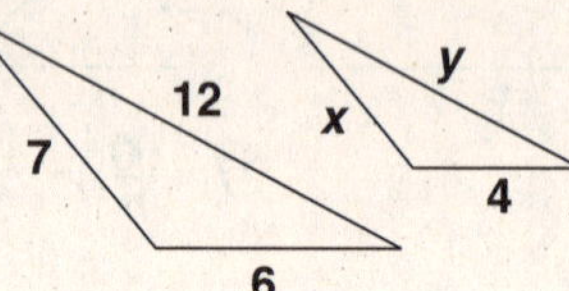

9. 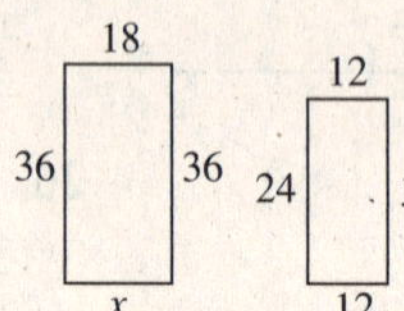

____

____

____

10. 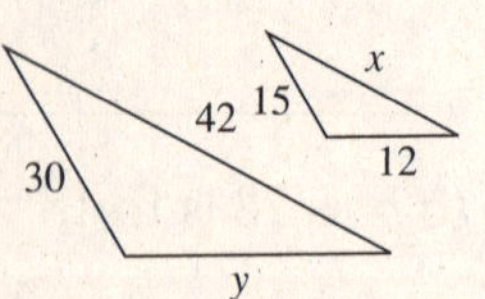

11. 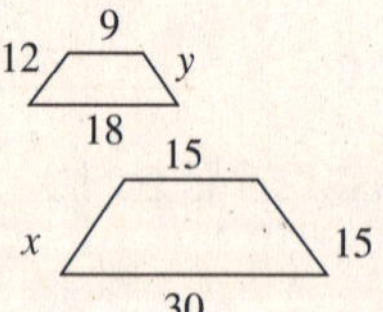

12. 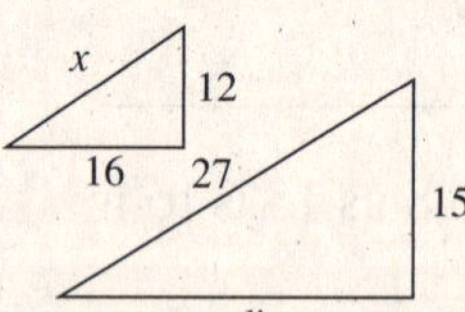

____

____

____

13. 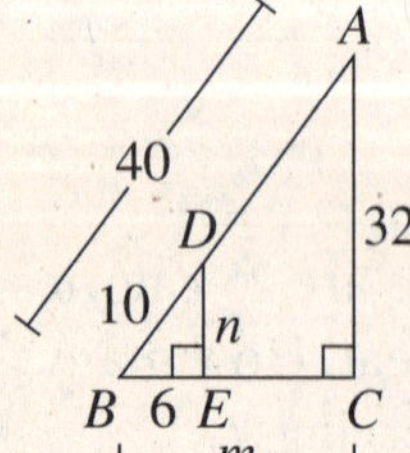

14. 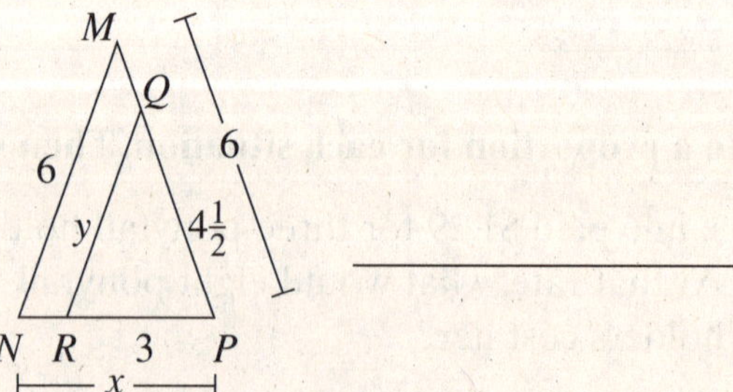

____

____

Solve.

15. A rock show is being televised. The lead singer, who is 75 inches tall, is 15 inches tall on a TV monitor. The image of the bass player is 13 inches tall on the monitor. How tall is the bass player?

16. A 42-inch-long guitar is 10.5-feet-long on a stadium screen. A drum is 21 inches wide. How wide is the image on the stadium screen?

____

____

Practice 5-6

Similarity Transformations

Graph the coordinates of the quadrilateral *ABCD*. Find the coordinates of its image *A'B'C'D'* after a dilation with the given scale factor.

1. $A(2, -2)$, $B(3, 2)$, $C(-3, 2)$, $D(-2, -2)$; scale factor 2

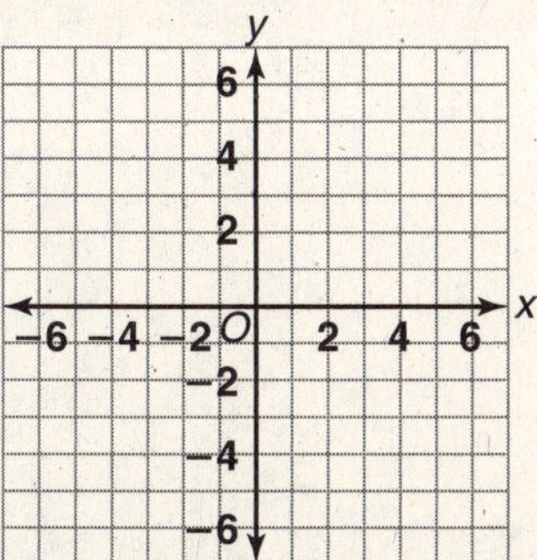

2. $A(6, 3)$, $B(0, 6)$, $C(-6, 2)$, $D(-6, -5)$; scale factor $\frac{1}{2}$

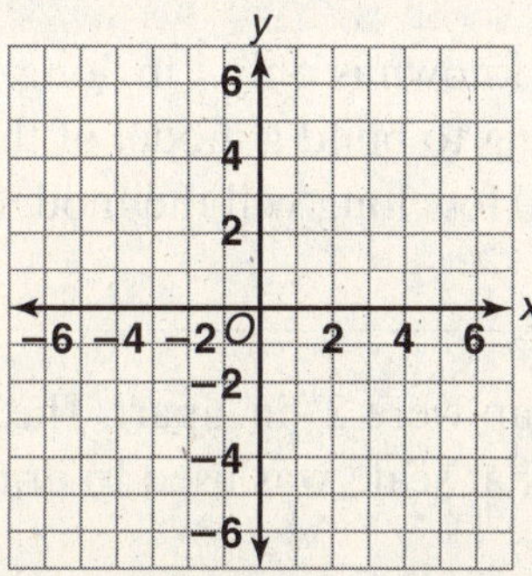

Quadrilateral *A'B'C'D'* is a dilation of quadrilateral *ABCD*. Find the scale factor. Classify each dilation as an enlargement or a reduction.

3.

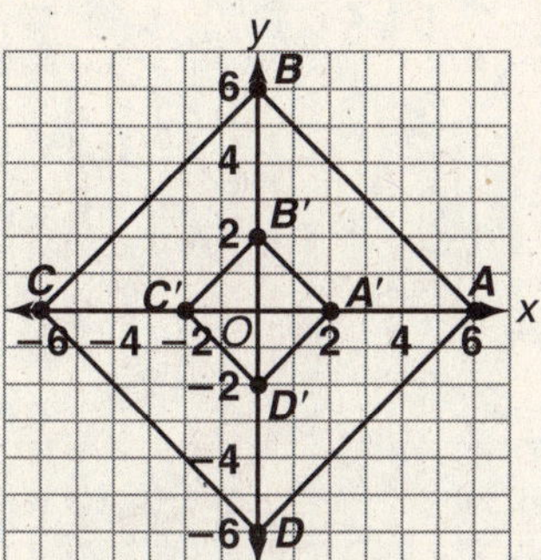

4.

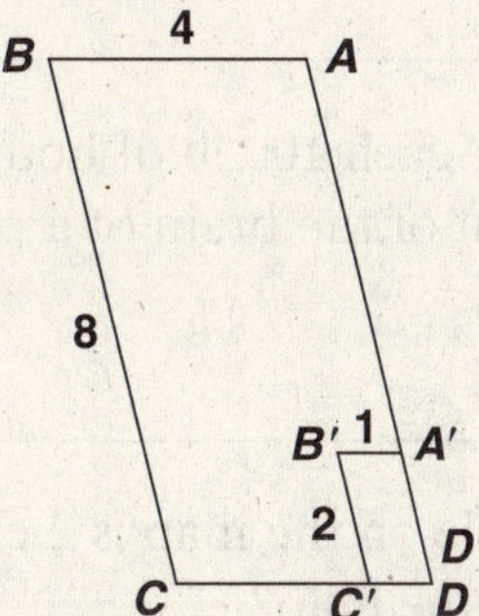

5.

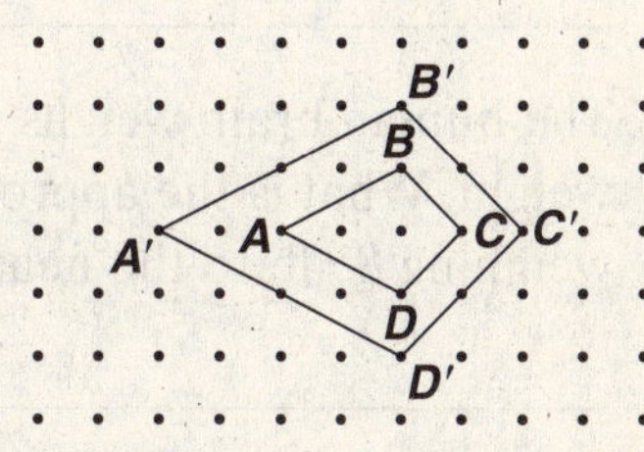

_______________   _______________   _______________

6. A triangle has coordinates $A(-2, -2)$, $B(4, -2)$, and $C(1, 1)$.
Graph its image $A'B'C'$ after a dilation with scale factor $\frac{3}{2}$.
Give the coordinates of $A'B'C'$, and the ratio of the areas of the figures $A'B'C'$ and ABC.

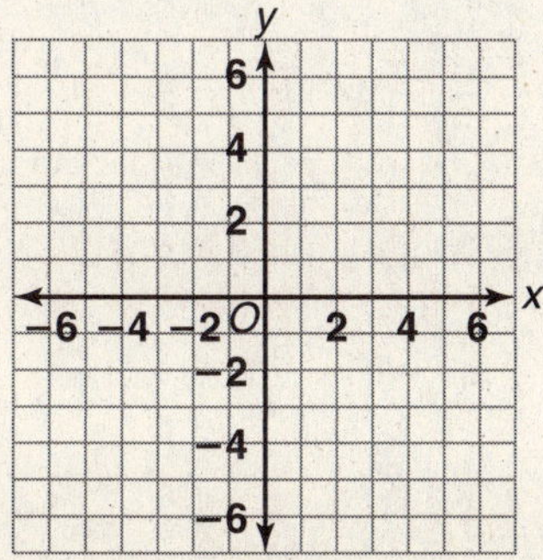

Practice 5-7

Solve each problem.

1. A scale model of a whale is being built. The actual length of the whale is 65 ft. The scale of the model is 2 in. : 3 ft. What will be the length of the model?

   ____

2. The smallest frog known is only $\frac{1}{2}$ in. long. A local science museum is planning to build a model of the frog. The scale used will be 3 in. : $\frac{1}{4}$ in. How long will the model be?

   ____

3. Two cities on a map were $2\frac{1}{4}$ in. apart. The cities are actually 56.25 mi apart. What scale was used to draw the map?

   ____

4. Four ounces of a certain perfume cost $20.96. How much would six ounces of perfume cost?

   ____

5. The human brain weighs about 1 lb for each 100 lb of body weight. What is the approximate weight of the brain of a person weighing 85 lb to the nearest ounce?

   ____

6. Two towns are 540 km apart. If the scale on the map is 2 cm to 50 km, how far apart are the towns on the map?

   ____

7. Cans of tuna cost $1.59 for $6\frac{1}{2}$ oz. At that rate, how much would 25 oz of tuna cost?

   ____

8. Students are building a model of a volcano. The volcano is about 8,000 ft tall. The students want the model to be 18 in. tall. What scale should they use?

   ____

9. A certain shade of paint requires 3 parts of blue to 2 parts of yellow to 1 part of red. If 18 gal of that shade of paint are needed, how many gal of blue are needed?

   ____

Practice 5-8

Similarity and Indirect Measurement

In each figure, find *x*.

1.

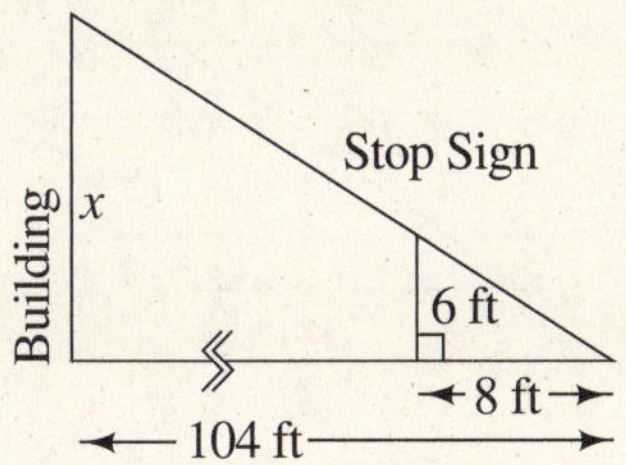

____

2.

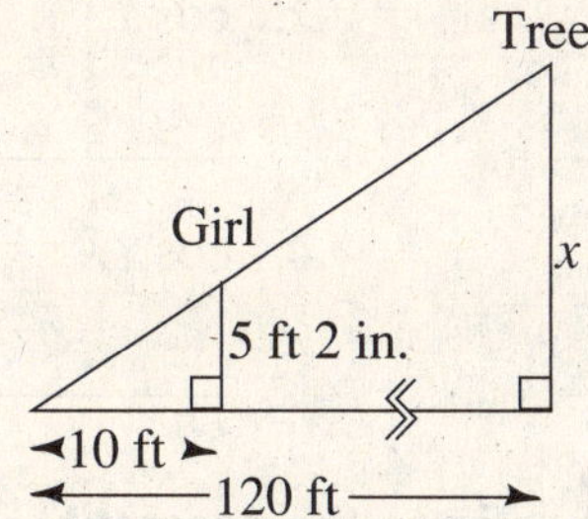

____

3.

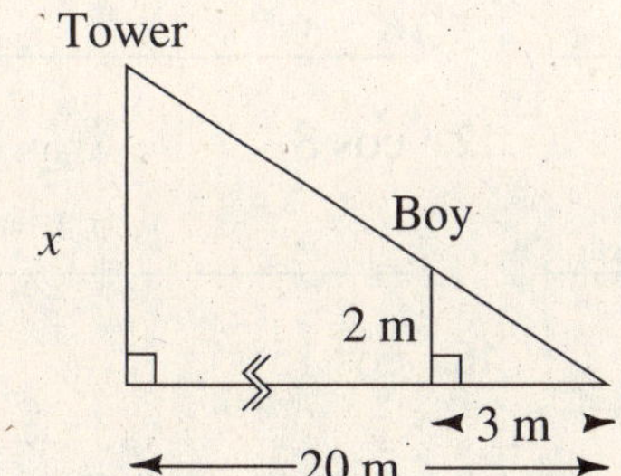

____

4.

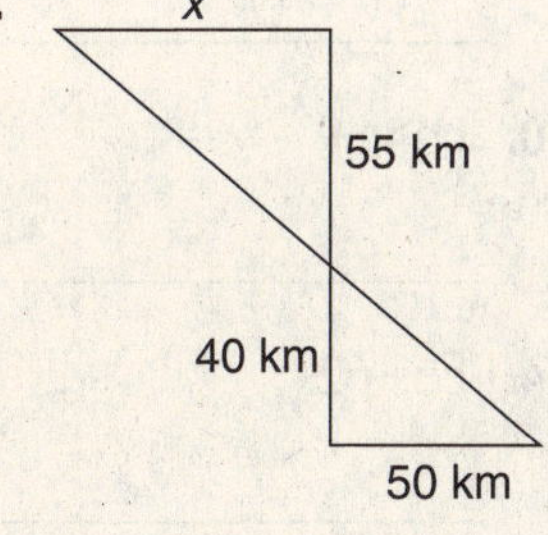

____

5.

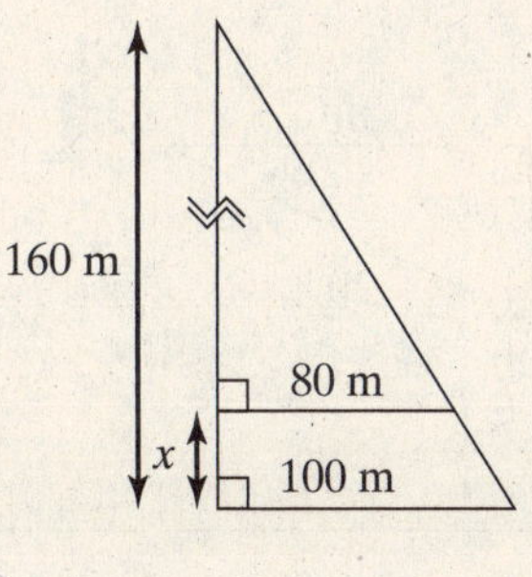

____

6.

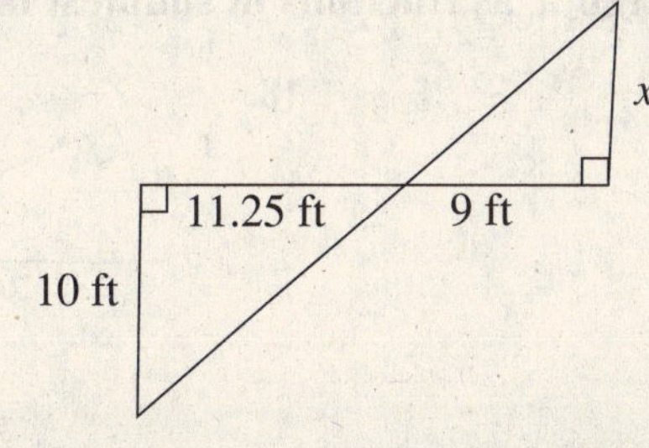

____

Solve.

7. An office building 55 ft tall casts a shadow 30 ft long. How tall is a person standing nearby who casts a shadow 3 ft long?

____

8. A 20-ft pole casts a shadow 12 ft long. How tall is a nearby building that casts a shadow 20 ft long?

____

9. A fire tower casts a shadow 30 ft long. A nearby tree casts a shadow 8 ft long. How tall is the fire tower if the tree is 20 ft tall?

____

10. A house casts a shadow 12 m long. A tree in the yard casts a shadow 8 m long. How tall is the tree if the house is 20 m tall?

____

Practice 5-9

The Sine and Cosine Ratios

Find each trigonometric ratio as a fraction in simplest form.

1. $\sin J$

____

2. $\cos J$

____

3. $\sin L$

____

4. $\cos L$

____

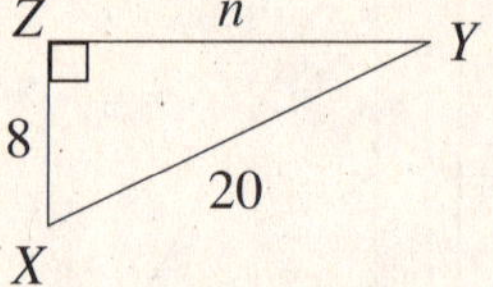

Find each sine or cosine ratio to the nearest ten-thousandth.

5. $\sin 48°$

____

6. $\cos 57°$

____

7. $\sin 18°$

____

8. $\cos 18°$

____

9. $\sin 89°$

____

10. $\cos 89°$

____

11. $\sin 37°$

____

12. $\cos 8°$

____

13. $\sin 54°$

____

14. $\cos 62°$

____

15. $\sin 75°$

____

16. $\cos 15°$

____

Use the Pythagorean theorem to find n in Exercise 17–19. Then write $\sin X$, $\cos X$, and $\tan X$ as fractions in simplest form.

17.

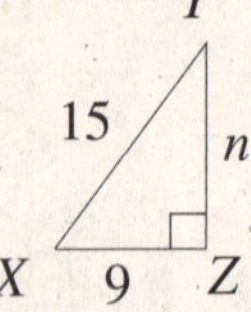

18.

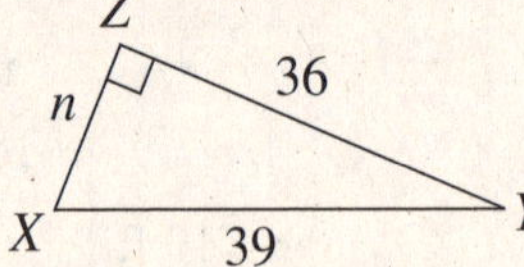

19.

____

____

Answer each question.

20. A man on a 135-ft vertical cliff looks down at an angle of 16° and sees his friend. How far away is the man from his friend? How far is the friend from the base of the cliff?

____

21. A 12-ft tree fell against a house during a thunderstorm. The tree formed a 56° angle with the ground. How far away from the house does the base of the tree stand?

____

Practice 6-1

Fractions, Decimals, and Percents

Use mental math to write each decimal as a percent.

1. 0.95 _________ **2.** 0.06 _________ **3.** 0.004 _________ **4.** 0.27 _________

5. 0.63 _________ **6.** 0.005 _________ **7.** 1.4 _________ **8.** 2.57 _________

Choose a calculator or a paper and pencil to write each fraction as a percent. Round to the nearest tenth of a percent.

9. $\frac{4}{5}$ _________ **10.** $\frac{7}{10}$ _________ **11.** $\frac{5}{6}$ _________ **12.** $4\frac{1}{2}$ _________

13. $\frac{5}{8}$ _________ **14.** $\frac{1}{15}$ _________ **15.** $\frac{9}{25}$ _________ **16.** $1\frac{7}{8}$ _________

17. $\frac{1}{6}$ _________ **18.** $\frac{11}{12}$ _________ **19.** $\frac{1}{20}$ _________ **20.** $3\frac{9}{20}$ _________

Use mental math to write each percent as a decimal.

21. 70% _________ **22.** 10% _________ **23.** 800% _________ **24.** 37% _________

25. 2.6% _________ **26.** 234% _________ **27.** 9% _________ **28.** $3\frac{1}{2}$% _________

Write each percent as a fraction in simplest form.

29. 10% _________ **30.** 47% _________ **31.** $5\frac{1}{2}$% _________ **32.** 473% _________

33. 15% _________ **34.** 92% _________ **35.** $3\frac{1}{4}$% _________ **36.** 548% _________

37. 85% _________ **38.** 42% _________ **39.** 70% _________ **40.** 150% _________

Solve.

41. There are twelve pairs of cranial nerves connected to the brain. Ten of these pairs are related to sight, smell, taste, and sound. What percent of the pairs are related to sight, smell, taste, and sound?

____

42. If a person weighs 150 lb, then calcium makes up 3 lb of that person's weight. What percent of a person's weight does calcium make up?

____

43. A quality control inspector found that 7 out of every 200 flashlights produced were defective. What percent of the flashlights were *not* defective?

____

44. In 1992, 80 varieties of reptiles were on the endangered species list. Eight of these were found only in the United States. What percent of the reptiles on the endangered species list were found only in the United States?

____

Practice 6-2

Estimating With Percents

Estimate.

1. 6% of 140

2. 18.9% of 44

3. 61% of 180

4. 5.1% of 81

5. $16\frac{1}{2}$% of 36

6. 81% of 241

7. 67% of 300

8. 51% of 281

9. 62.9% of 400

10. 76% of 600

11. 88% of 680

12. 37% of 481

13. 19.1% of 380

14. 41% of 321

15. 33% of 331

16. 83% of 453

17. 76.3% of 841

18. 67.1% of 486

19. 84% of 93

20. 0.3% of 849

21. 81.2% of 974

22. 0.87% of 250

23. 57.9% of 500

24. 62% of 400

Estimate.

25. Of the 307 species of mammals on the endangered list in 1992, 12.1% of them were found only in the United States. Estimate the number of mammal species in the United States that were on the endangered list.

26. In 1990, 19% of the people of Mali lived in urban settings. If the population that year was 9,200,000, estimate the number of people who lived in urban settings.

27. Of the 1,267 students at the school, 9.8% live within walking distance of school. Estimate the number of students within walking distance.

28. Of the 1,267 students at the school, 54.6% have to ride the bus. About how many students have to ride the bus?

Practice 6-3

Percents and Proportions

Write a proportion that will help you answer the problem. Then solve each problem.

1. What percent is 21 of 50?

2. What is 45% of 72?

3. 83 is 70% of what number?

4. 45 is what percent of 65?

Use a proportion to solve each problem.

5. 78% of 58 is __________.

6. 86 is 12% of __________.

7. 90 is __________ of 65.

8. 40 is 17% of __________.

9. 57 is 31% of __________.

10. 280% of __________ is 418.

11. 53% of 92 is __________.

12. 56 is 25% of __________.

13. 51 is __________ of 14.

14. What percent of 42 is 18?

15. 58 is 40% of what number?

16. What is 70% of 93?

17. 240 is what percent of 150?

18. What percent of 16 is 40?

19. 65 is 60% of what number?

20. What is 175% of 48?

21. 210 is what percent of 70?

22. What percent of 56 is 7?

23. 68 is 50% of what number?

24. What is 63% of 148?

25. 215 is what percent of 400?

Solve.

26. In 1990, the population of El Paso, Texas, was 515,342. Of this population, 69% were of Hispanic origin. How many people were of Hispanic origin?

27. Bangladesh covers 55,598 mi^2. Of this land, 2,224 mi^2 are meadows and pastures. What percent of the land is meadow and pasture?

Practice 6-4

Percents and Equations

Use an equation to solve each problem. Round to the nearest tenth.

1. What percent of 80 is 25? _____________
2. 8.6 is 5% of what number? _____________
3. What is 140% of 85? _____________
4. 70 is what percent of 120? _____________
5. What percent of 90 is 42? _____________
6. 18.4 is what percent of 10? _____________
7. 56% of what number is 82? _____________
8. Find 93% of 150. _____________
9. 30% of what number is 120? _____________
10. What percent of 420 is 7? _____________
11. 79 is what percent of 250? _____________
12. 9.1 is 3% of what number? _____________
13. What is 94% of 260? _____________
14. 45 is what percent of 18? _____________
15. What percent of 280 is 157? _____________
16. 20.7 is what percent of 8? _____________
17. 114% of what number is 75? _____________
18. Find 72% of 18,495. _____________
19. 75% of what number is 200? _____________
20. What percent of 940 is 15? _____________
21. 80 is what percent of 450? _____________
22. Find 65% of 2,190. _____________
23. 90 is what percent of 40? _____________
24. 45 is what percent of 900? _____________
25. 82 is 90% of what number? _____________
26. 50 is 120% of what number? _____________

Solve.

27. In a recent survey, 216 people, or 54% of the sample, said they usually went to a family restaurant when they went out to eat. How many people were surveyed?

28. In a school survey, 248 students, or 32% of the sample, said they worked part time during the summer. How many students were surveyed?

29. Juliet sold a house for $112,000. What percent commission did she receive if she earned $6,720?

30. Jason earns $200 per week plus 8% commission on his sales. How much were his sales last week if Jason earned $328?

31. Stella makes 2% royalties on a book she wrote. How much money did her book earn in sales last year if she made $53,000 in royalties?

32. Linda earns $40 base pay per week, plus 10% commission on all sales. What were her sales if she made $112 in one week?

33. Kevin sold a house for $57,000. His fee, or sales commission, for selling the house was $2,679. What percent of the price of the house was Kevin's commission?

34. Marik agreed to pay a realtor 6.5% commission for selling his house. If the house sold for $68,900, how much does Marik have after paying the realtor's commission?

Name _______________________ Class _______________________ Date _______________________

Practice 6-5

Find each percent of change. Label your answer as increase or decrease. Round to the nearest tenth of a percent.

1. 15 to 20

____

2. 18 to 10

____

3. 10 to 7.5

____

4. 86 to 120

____

5. 17 to 34

____

6. 32 to 24

____

7. 27 to 38

____

8. 40 to 10

____

9. 8 to 10

____

10. 43 to 86

____

11. 100 to 23

____

12. 846 to 240

____

13. 130 to 275

____

14. 193 to 270

____

15. 436 to 118

____

16. 457 to 318

____

17. 607 to 812

____

18. 500 to 118

____

19. 346 to 843

____

20. 526 to 1,000

____

21. 1,000 to 526

____

22. 489 to 751

____

23. 286 to 781

____

24. 846 to 957

____

Solve.

25. In 1995, the price of a laser printer was $1,299. In 2002, the price of the same type of printer had dropped to $499. Find the percent of decrease.

____

26. The amount won in harness racing in 1991 was $1.238 million. In 1992, the amount was $1.38 million. What was the percent of increase?

____

27. In 1980, there were about 3 million people in Chicago. In 1990, the population was about 2.8 million people. Find the percent of decrease in the population of Chicago.

____

28. Caryn was 58 in. tall last year. This year she is 61 in. tall. What is the percent of increase in her height?

____

29. Last month, Dave weighed 175 lb. This month he weighs 164 lb. What is the percent of decrease in Dave's weight?

____

30. Between the ages of 1 and 10 a life insurance policy costs $3.84 per month. At the age of 11, the policy increases to $6.12 per month. Find the percent of increase.

____

Practice 6-6

Markup and Discount

Find each selling price. Round to the nearest cent.

1. cost: $10.00
markup rate: 60%

____

2. cost: $12.50
markup rate: 50%

____

3. cost: $15.97
markup rate: 75%

____

4. cost: $21.00
markup rate: 100%

____

5. cost: $25.86
markup rate: 70%

____

6. cost: $32.48
markup rate: 110%

____

7. cost: $47.99
markup rate: 160%

____

8. cost: $87.90
markup rate: 80%

____

9. cost: $95.90
markup rate: 112%

____

10. cost: $120.00
markup rate: 56%

____

11. cost: $150.97
markup rate: 65%

____

12. cost: $2,000.00
markup rate: 95%

____

Find each sale price. Round to the nearest cent.

13. regular price: $10.00
discount rate: 10%

____

14. regular price: $12.00
discount rate: 15%

____

15. regular price: $18.95
discount rate: 20%

____

16. regular price: $20.95
discount rate: 15%

____

17. regular price: $32.47
discount rate: 20%

____

18. regular price: $39.99
discount rate: 25%

____

19. regular price: $42.58
discount rate: 30%

____

20. regular price: $53.95
discount rate: 35%

____

21. regular price: $82.99
discount rate: 50%

____

22. regular price: $126.77
discount rate: 62%

____

23. regular price: $250.98
discount rate: 70%

____

24. regular price: $2,000.00
discount rate: 15%

____

Find each store's cost. Round to the nearest cent.

25. selling price: $55
markup rate: 20%

____

26. selling price: $25.50
markup rate: 45%

____

27. selling price: $79.99
markup rate: 30%

____

28. selling price: $19.95
markup rate: 75%

____

29. selling price: $95
markup rate: 25%

____

30. selling price: $64.49
markup rate: 10%

____

Practice 6-7

Problem Solving: Write an Equation

Use any strategy to solve each problem. Show your work.

1. On a map, the distance between Wauseon and Archbold is 8 cm. What is the actual distance between the cities if 2.5 cm = 1 mi?

   ____

2. The drama club sold adult tickets for $8 and children's tickets for $5. For the final performance a total of 226 tickets were sold for a total of $1,670. How many adult tickets were sold for the performance?

   ____

3. The Caston's budget is shown at the right. They just learned that their house payment will be increased by $120. Their income will be no more than it is now, so they plan on reducing each of the other categories by an equal amount. How much money will they then be able to budget for bills?

Caston's Budget	
Item	Amount
House	$750
Food	$400
Bills	$350
Other	$140

   ____

4. Rhonda added 140 to one third of a number for a result of 216. What is the number?

   ____

5. The sum of three consecutive integers is 228. What are the integers?

   ____

6. Angie has an equal number of dimes and quarters. The total value of her coins is $3.50. How many dimes does she have?

   ____

7. How many ways can you arrange the letters A, B, C, and D in a row if A and B are never next to each other?

   ____

8. One month, Meredith's parents doubled her monthly allowance. The next month, they increased her allowance by $3. The next month, they cut her allowance in half. Is her allowance more or less now than her original allowance? By how much?

   ____

Practice 6-8

Simple and Compound Interest

Find the final balance in each account. Round your answers to the nearest cent.

1. $800 at 4.25% simple interest for 6 years

2. $800 at 6% compounded annually for 4 years

3. $250 at 5% simple interest for 3 years

4. $900 at 8% simple interest for 1 year

5. $1,250 at 5% simple interest for 2 years

6. $1,250 at $4\frac{1}{2}$% compounded annually for 3 years

7. $1,500 at 4% compounded annually for 4 years

8. $1,750 at 5% simple interest for 2 years

9. $2,000 at 6% simple interest for 3 years

10. $2,000 at 6% compounded annually for 3 years

11. $2,500 at 6% compounded annually for 3 years

12. $4,000 at 6% compounded annually for 3 years

13. $5,000 at 5% simple interest for 10 years

14. $6,000 at 5% simple interest for 6 years

15. $5,000 at 5% compounded annually for 10 years

16. $6,000 at 5% compounded annually for 8 years

Solve.

17. Bill invests $500. How much will it grow to in 20 years at 6% compounded annually?

18. In Exercise 17, how much less will Bill have in the account if the interest is simple interest?

19. Which earns more compound interest, $1,000 at 5% for 10 years or $1,000 at 10% for 5 years? How much more?

20. Which earns more simple interest, $1,000 at 5% for 10 years or $1,000 at 10% for 5 years? How much more?

Practice 6-9

Probability

A dart is thrown at the game board shown. Find each probability.

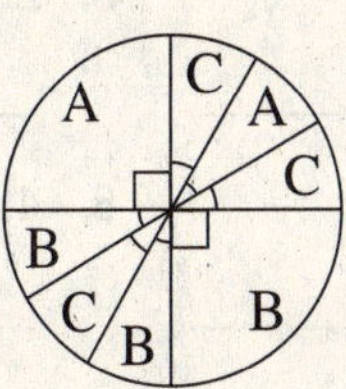

1. $P(A)$ _______   2. $P(B)$ _______

3. $P(C)$ _______   4. $P(A \text{ or } B)$ _______

5. $P(B \text{ or } C)$ _______   6. $P(A, B, \text{ or } C)$ _______

A bag of uninflated balloons contains 10 red, 12 blue, 15 yellow, and 8 green balloons. A balloon is drawn at random. Find each probability.

7. $P(\text{red})$ _______   8. $P(\text{blue})$ _______   9. $P(\text{yellow})$ _______   10. $P(\text{green})$ _______

11. What is the probability of picking a balloon that is not yellow?

____

12. What is the probability of picking a balloon that is not red?

____

Solve.

13. **a.** You are given a ticket for the weekly drawing each time you enter the grocery store. Last week you were in the store once. There are 1,200 tickets in the box. Find the probability of you winning.

____

b. Find the probability of you winning if you were in the store three times last week and there are 1,200 tickets in the box.

____

14. A cheese tray contains slices of Swiss cheese and cheddar cheese. If you randomly pick a slice of cheese, $P(\text{Swiss}) = 0.45$. Find $P(\text{cheddar})$. If there are 200 slices of cheese, how many slices of Swiss cheese are on the tray?

____

15. **a.** Make a table to find the sample space for tossing two coins.

b. Find the probability that you get one head and one tail when tossing two coins.

____

Practice 7-1

Scientific Notation

Write each number in scientific notation.

1. 45

2. 250

3. 90

4. 200

5. 670

6. 4,100

7. 500

8. 3,000

9. 43,200

10. 97,100

11. 38,050

12. 90,200

13. 480,000

14. 960,000

15. 8,750,000

16. 407,000

Write each number in standard form.

17. 3.1×10^1

18. 8.07×10^2

19. 4.96×10^3

20. 8.073×10^2

21. 4.501×10^4

22. 9.7×10^6

23. 8.3×10^7

24. 3.42×10^4

25. 2.86×10^5

26. 3.58×10^6

27. 8.1×10^1

28. 9.071×10^2

29. 4.83×10^9

30. 2.73×10^8

31. 2.57×10^5

32. 8.09×10^4

Order each set of numbers from least to greatest.

33. $8.9 \times 10^2, 6.3 \times 10^3, 2.1 \times 10^4, 7.8 \times 10^5$

34. $2.1 \times 10^4, 2.12 \times 10^3, 3.46 \times 10^5, 2.112 \times 10^2$

35. $8.93 \times 10^3, 7.8 \times 10^2, 7.84 \times 10^3, 8.915 \times 10^4$

Write each number in scientific notation.

36. The eye's retina contains about 130 million light-sensitive cells.

37. A mulberry silkworm can spin a single thread that measures up to 3,900 ft in length.

Practice 7-2

Exponents and Multiplication

Write each expression using a single exponent.

1. $3^2 \cdot 3^5$

2. $1^3 \cdot 1^4$

3. $5^4 \cdot 5^3$

4. $a^1 \cdot a^2$

5. $(-y)^3 \cdot (-y)^2$

6. $-z^3 \cdot z^9$

7. $(3x) \cdot (3x)$

8. $4.5^8 \cdot 4.5^2$

9. $(5x) \cdot (5x)^3$

10. $3^3 \cdot 3 \cdot 3^4$

11. $x^2y \cdot xy^2$

12. $5x^2 \cdot x^6 \cdot x^3$

Find each product. Write the answers in scientific notation.

13. $(3 \times 10^4)(5 \times 10^6)$

14. $(9 \times 10^7)(3 \times 10^2)$

15. $(7 \times 10^2)(6 \times 10^4)$

16. $(3 \times 10^{10})(4 \times 10^5)$

17. $(4 \times 10^5)(7 \times 10^8)$

18. $(9.1 \times 10^6)(3 \times 10^9)$

19. $(8.4 \times 10^9)(5 \times 10^7)$

20. $(5 \times 10^3)(4 \times 10^6)$

21. $(7.2 \times 10^8)(2 \times 10^3)$

22. $(1.4 \times 10^5)(4 \times 10^{11})$

Replace each __?__ with =, <, or >.

23. 3^8 __?__ $3 \cdot 3^7$

24. 49 __?__ $7^2 \cdot 7^2$

25. $5^3 \cdot 5^4$ __?__ 25^2

26. Double the number 4.6×10^{15}. Write the answer in scientific notation.

27. Triple the number 2.3×10^3. Write the answer in scientific notation.

Practice 7-3

Exponents and Division

Simplify each expression.

1. 8^{-2} **2.** $(-3)^0$ **3.** 5^{-1} **4.** 18^0

_______   _______   _______   _______

5. 2^{-5} **6.** 3^{-3} **7.** 2^{-3} **8.** 5^{-2}

_______   _______   _______   _______

9. $\dfrac{4^4}{4}$ **10.** $8^6 \div 8^8$ **11.** $\dfrac{(-3)^6}{(-3)^8}$ **12.** $\dfrac{8^4}{8^0}$

_______   _______   _______   _______

3. $1^{15} \div 1^{18}$ **14.** $7 \div 7^4$ **15.** $\dfrac{(-4)^8}{(-4)^4}$ **16.** $\dfrac{10^9}{10^{12}}$

_______   _______   _______   _______

$\dfrac{7^5}{3}$ **18.** $8^4 \div 8^2$ **19.** $\dfrac{(-3)^5}{(-3)^8}$ **20.** $\dfrac{6^7}{6^8}$

_______   _______   _______   _______

22. $\dfrac{g^9}{g^{15}}$ **23.** $x^{16} \div x^7$ **24.** $v^{20} \div v^{25}$

_______   _______   _______

Complete each equation.

25. $\dfrac{1}{3^5} = 3^{\underline{\,?\,}}$ **26.** $\dfrac{1}{(-2)^7} = (-2)^{\underline{\,?\,}}$ **27.** $\dfrac{1}{x^2} = x^{\underline{\,?\,}}$ **28.** $\dfrac{1}{-125} = (-5)^{\underline{\,?\,}}$

_______   _______   _______   _______

29. $\dfrac{1}{1{,}000} = 10^{\underline{\,?\,}}$ **30.** $\dfrac{5^{10}}{?} = 5^5$ **31.** $\dfrac{z^{?}}{z^8} = z^{-3}$ **32.** $\dfrac{q^5}{?} = q^{-7}$

_______   _______   _______   _______

Write each number in scientific notation.

33. 0.0007 **34.** 0.00000001 **35.** 0.000901

_______   _______   _______

36. 0.0000000091 **37.** 0.0000000001 **38.** 0.000032

_______   _______   _______

39. Write each term as a power of 4, and write the next three terms
of the sequence 256, 64, 16, 4, ...

____

Practice 7-4

Power Rules

Write each expression using one base and one exponent.

1. $(5^3)^{-6}$

2. $(-9^4)^{-2}$

3. $(d^5)^6$

4. $(8^{-3})^{-9}$

5. $(4^{-3}, 4^{-2}, 4^{-1})^{-4}$

6. $(y^8)^{-6}$

7. $(v^3, v^6, v^9)^2$

8. $(k^{-7})^{-5}$

9. $((n^3)^2)^5$

10. $((a^2)^2)^2$

Simplify each expression.

11. $(xyz)^6$

12. $(10^2 \cdot x^7)^3$

13. $(7y^8)^2$

14. $(t^2 \cdot t^4)^5$

15. $(4g)^3$

16. $(x^5 y^4)^8$

Use >, <, or = to complete each statement.

17. $7^3 \cdot 7^3 \ \underline{\ ?\ } \ (7^3)^3$

18. $(6^{-2} \cdot 6^5)^3 \ \underline{\ ?\ } \ (6^3)^2$

19. $(4^6)^0 \ \underline{\ ?\ } \ 4^6 \cdot 4^{-6}$

20. Find the area of a square whose side is 3×10^4 millimeters. Write the answer in scientific notation.

21. As of October 29, 2002 the Ijen volcano had an active crater with a radius of 1,100 ft. Using the formula for a circle $A = \pi r^2$ and 3.14 for π, what is the area of the crater?

Practice 7-5

Problem Solving: Write an Equation

The top 10 United States counties with the greatest population are shown in the table.

Rank (of 3,141 counties)	County Name	State	Census Population April 1, 1990	April 1, 2000
1	Los Angeles County	CA	8.9×10^6	9.6×10^6
2	Cook County	IL	5.1×10^6	5.4×10^6
3	Harris County	TX	2.8×10^6	3.4×10^6
4	Maricopa County	AZ	2.1×10^6	3.1×10^6
5	Orange County	CA	2.4×10^6	2.8×10^6
6	San Diego County	CA	2.5×10^6	2.8×10^6
7	Kings County	NY	2.3×10^6	2.5×10^6
	Miami-Dade County	FL	1.9×10^6	2.3×10^6
	Queens County	NY	2.0×10^6	2.2×10^6
	Dallas County	TX	1.9×10^6	2.2×10^6

…problem by writing an equation. Check your answer.

1. …the population of Pima County in Arizona is about 4 …than that of the population of Harris County in Texas. …the population of Pima County in 1999?

____

2. In 2000, what was the difference in population between Cook County and Queens County?

____

3. About how many times larger was Los Angeles County than Cook County in 1990?

____

4. In 2000, the population of Orange County in Florida was 896,344. How many more people lived in Miami-Dade County in 2000 than in Orange County?

____

____

5. The mayor of Kings County in New York expects the population to increase by about 10% from 2000 to 2010. How many people are predicted to populate that county in 2010?

____

Practice 7-6

Number Systems

Write the decimal value for each binary number.

1. 11011_2 **2.** 100110_2 **3.** 10001_2

_______________   _______________   _______________

4. 11010_2 **5.** 110010_2 **6.** 110111_2

_______________   _______________   _______________

7. 110011_2 **8.** 11110_2 **9.** 11100_2

_______________   _______________   _______________

10. 1011001_2 **11.** 1101010_2 **12.** 10001111_2

_______________   _______________   _______________

13. 10001110_2 **14.** 1111111_2 **15.** 1001010_2

_______________   _______________   _______________

Write each decimal number as a binary number.

16. 14   **17.** 22

_______________   _______________

18. 58   **19.** 63

_______________   _______________

20. 86   **21.** 102

_______________   _______________

22. 65   **23.** 101

_______________   _______________

The base-5 number system uses the digits 0, 1, 2, 3, and 4 with place values using powers of 5. Write the decimal value for each base-5 number.

24. 123_5 **25.** 222_5 **26.** 431_5

_______________   _______________   _______________

The hexadecimal (base-6) number system uses the digits 0, 1, 2, 3, 4, and 5 with place values using powers of 6. Write the decimal value for each hexadecimal number.

27. 111_6 **28.** 214_6 **29.** 152_6

_______________   _______________   _______________

Practice 8-1

Pairs of Angles

Name a pair of vertical angles and a pair of adjacent angles in each figure. Find $m\angle 1$.

1.

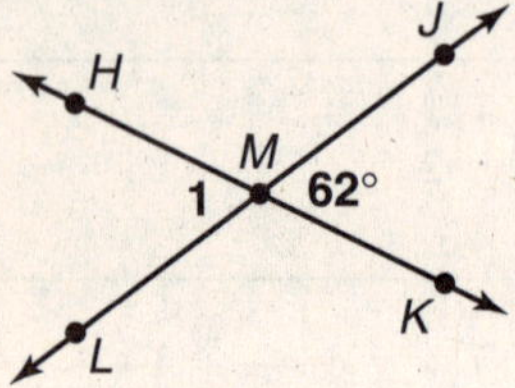

____

____

2.

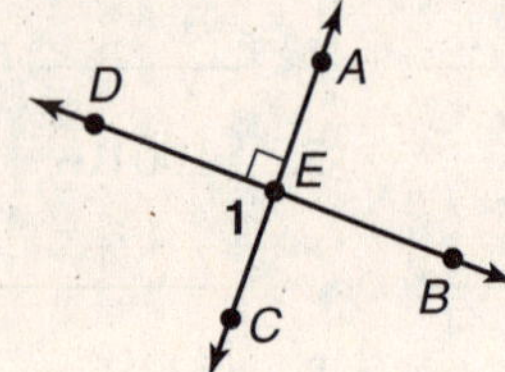

____

____

3.

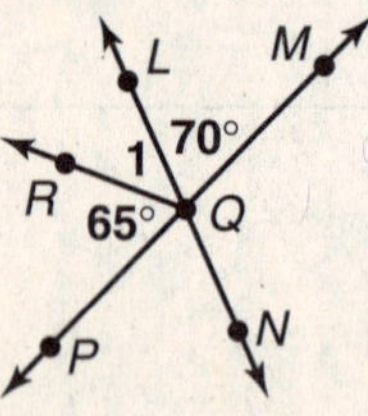

____

____

4.

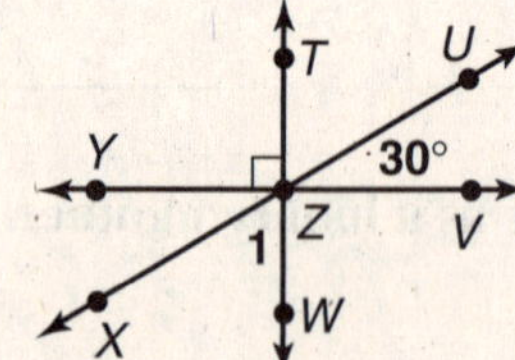

____

____

Find the measure of the supplement and the complement of each angle.

5. $10°$ **6.** $38°$ **7.** $42.5°$ **8.** $n°$

______________ ______________ ______________ ______________

Use the diagram at the right for Exercises 9–14. Decide whether each statement below is true or false.

9. $\angle GAF$ and $\angle BAC$ are vertical angles. ______________

10. $\angle EAF$ and $\angle EAD$ are adjacent angles. ______________

11. $\angle CAD$ is a supplement of $\angle DAF$. ______________

12. $\angle CAD$ is a complement of $\angle EAF$. ______________

13. $m\angle GAC = 90°$ ______________

14. $m\angle DAF = 109°$ ______________

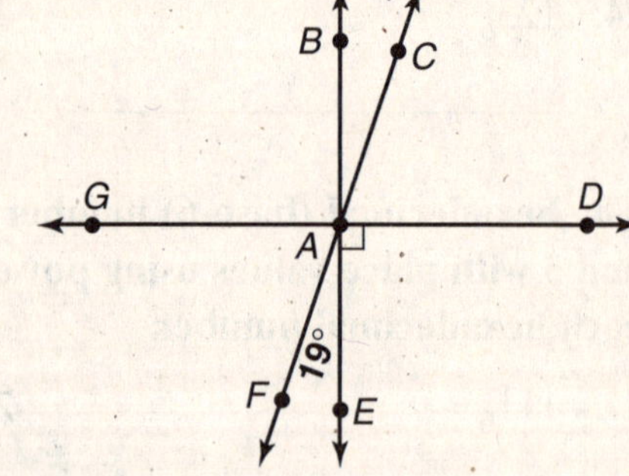

Practice 8-2

Angles and Parallel Lines

Identify each pair of angles as *vertical*, *adjacent*, *corresponding*, *alternate interior*, or *none of these*.

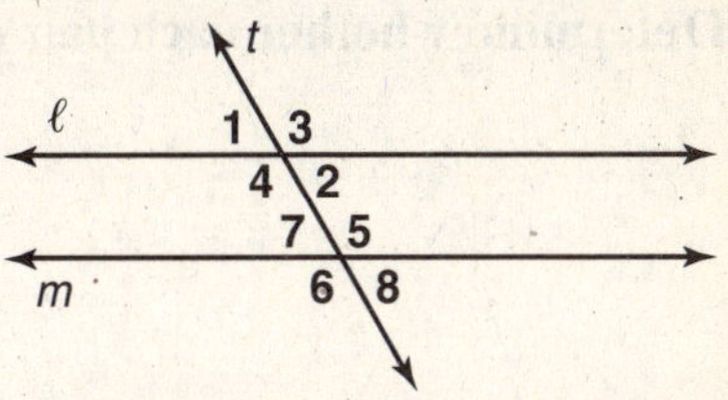

1. $\angle 7, \angle 5$

____

2. $\angle 1, \angle 2$

____

3. $\angle 1, \angle 5$

____

4. $\angle 1, \angle 7$

____

5. $\angle 4, \angle 7$

____

6. $\angle 4, \angle 5$

____

Use the diagrams at the right for Exercises 7 and 8.

7. Name four pairs of corresponding angles.

____

8. Name two pairs of alternate interior angles.

____

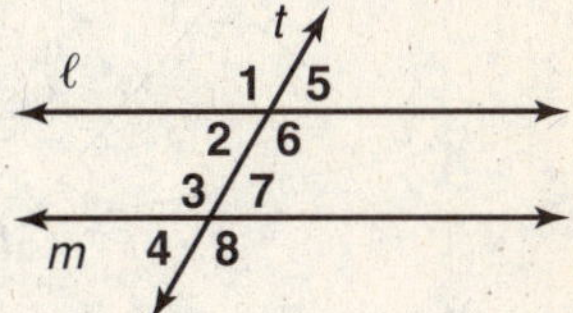

In each diagram below, $\ell \parallel m$. Find the measure of each numbered angle.

9.

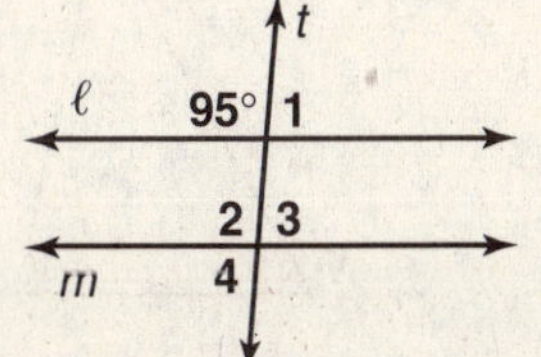

$m\angle 1 = $ _____________

$m\angle 2 = $ _____________

$m\angle 3 = $ _____________

$m\angle 4 = $ _____________

10.

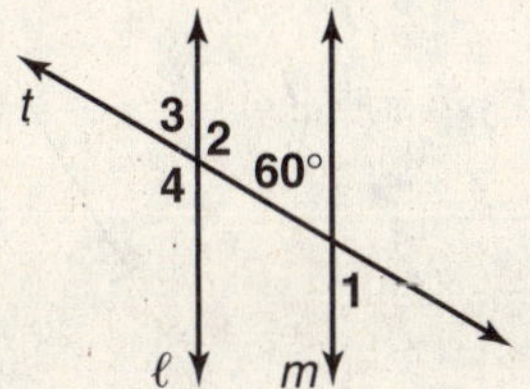

$m\angle 1 = $ _____________

$m\angle 2 = $ _____________

$m\angle 3 = $ _____________

$m\angle 4 = $ _____________

11.

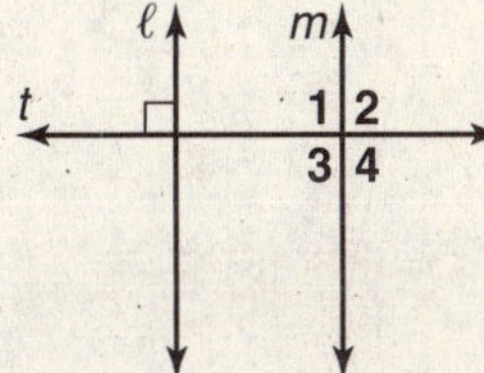

$m\angle 1 = $ _____________

$m\angle 2 = $ _____________

$m\angle 3 = $ _____________

$m\angle 4 = $ _____________

12. Use the figure at the right. Is line ℓ parallel to line m? Explain how you could use a protractor to support your conjecture.

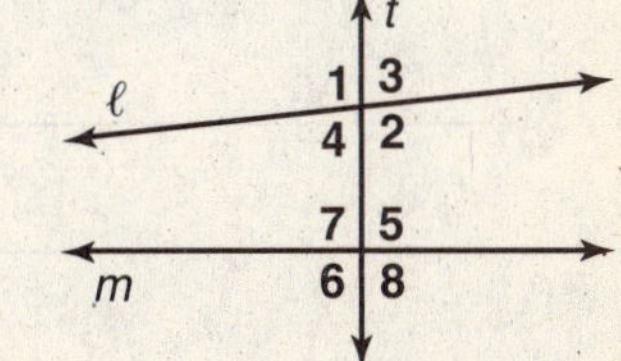

____

____

____

Practice 8-3   **Congruent Polygons**

Determine whether each pair of triangles is congruent. Explain.

1. 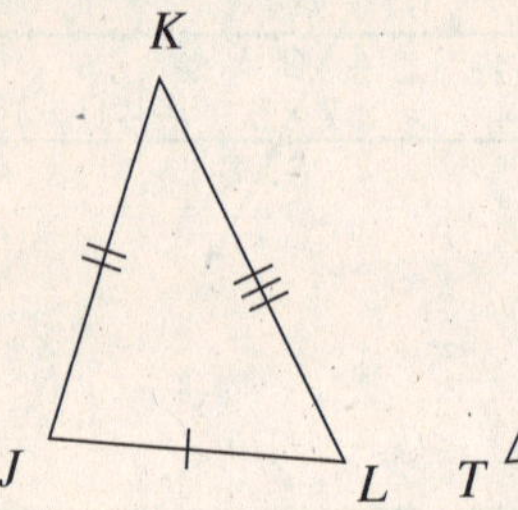 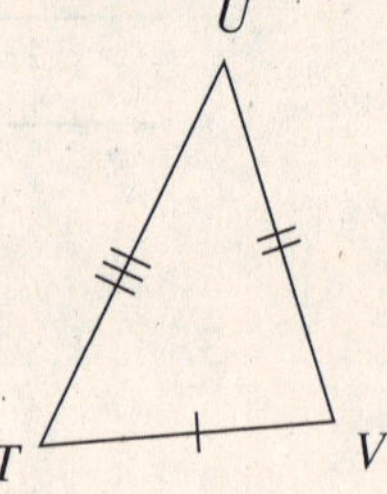

2. 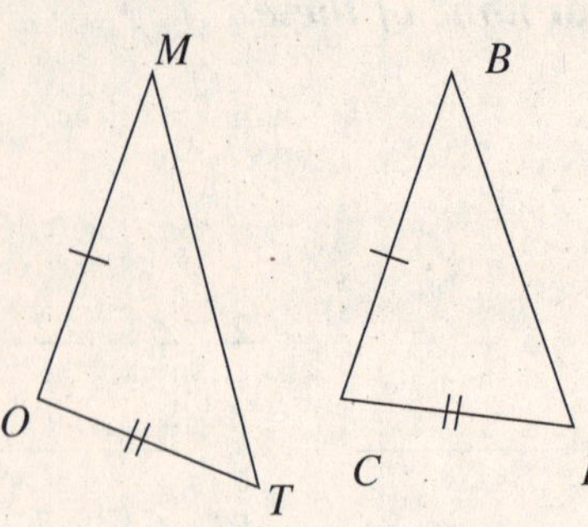

_______________________________   _______________________________

3. 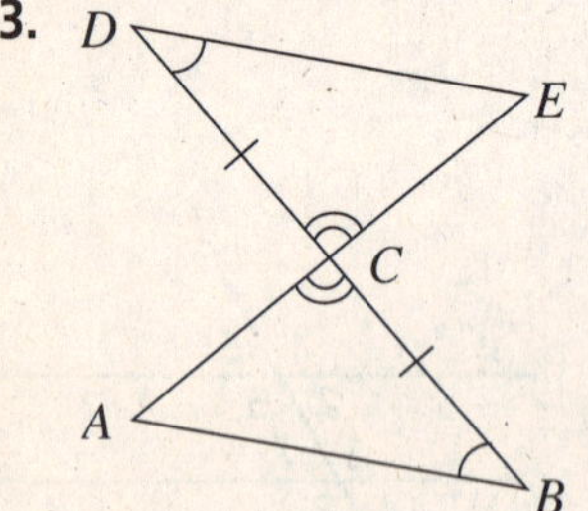

4. 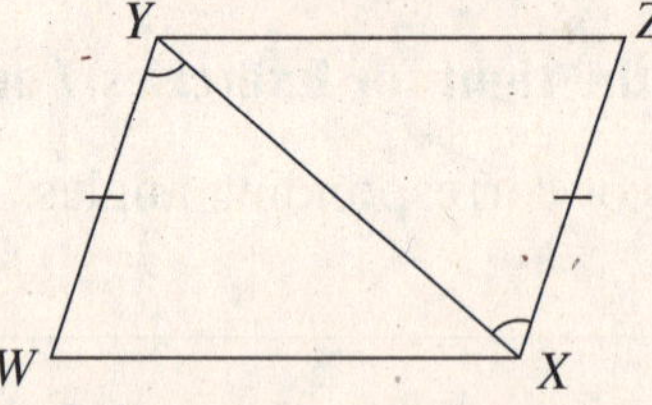

_______________________________   _______________________________

Determine if each triangle in Exercises 5–7 is congruent to △*XYZ* at the right.

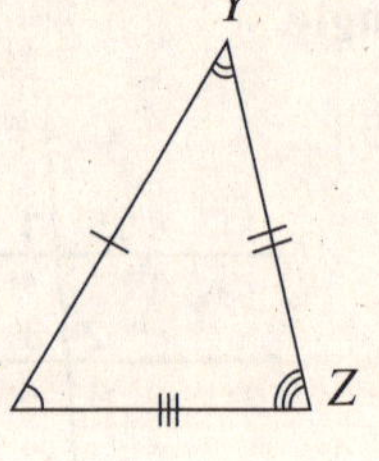

5. 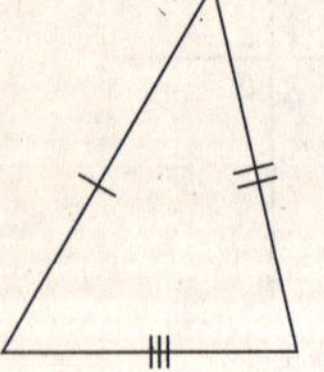   **6.** 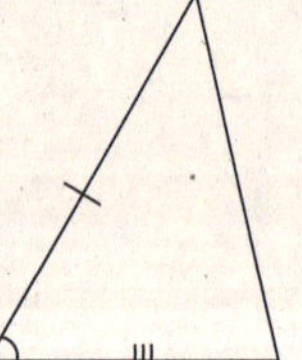   **7.** 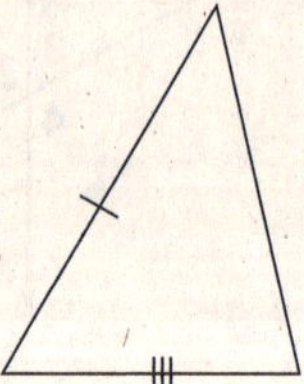

_______________   _______________   _______________

For Exercises 8–9, use the triangles at the right.

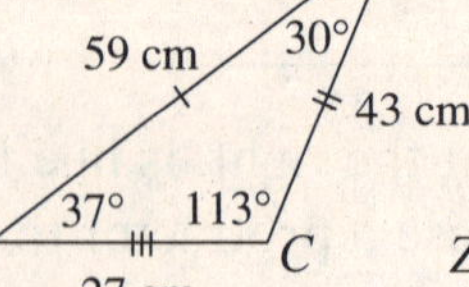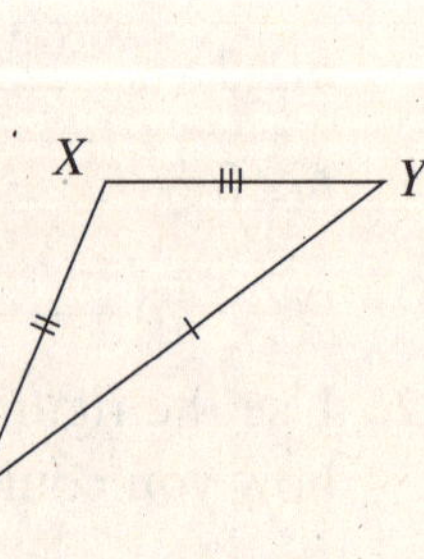

8. △*XYZ* ≅ _________________ by _________________

9. Find the missing measures for △*XYZ*.

____

____

Practice 8-4

Problem Solving: Solve a Simpler Problem and Look for a Pattern

Solve each problem by solving a simpler problem. Then look for a pattern.

1. A series of numbers can be represented by dots arranged in the pattern shown below. If the pattern continues in the same manner, what number is represented by the tenth figure?

   ____

2. Alma sent out 4 cards on Monday, 8 cards on Tuesday, 16 cards on Wednesday, and 28 cards on Thursday. If this pattern continues, how many cards did Alma send out on Saturday?

   ____

3. Find the next number in the pattern. 2, 2, 4, 6, 10, 16, 26, . . .

   ____

Choose a strategy or a combination of strategies to solve each problem.

4. Jen picked a number, added 9 to it, multiplied the sum by 8, and then subtracted 11. The result was 133. What number did Jen start with?

   ____

5. Ajani was offered a job in which he was paid $.01 the first day, $.02 the second day, $.04 the third day, $.08 the fourth day, and so on. On which day was Ajani first paid more than $100?

   ____

6. Bruno and Grete work in a flower shop. By noon, Bruno had made twice as many flower baskets as Grete. From noon to 3:00 P.M., Grete made 6 more baskets, while Bruno made only 1 more. At 5:00 P.M., Grete had made 10 more flower baskets, while Bruno had made only 3 more. At 5:00 P.M., Bruno had made a total of 4 fewer flower baskets than Grete made all day. How many flower baskets did each make in all?

   ____

7. Doug washes his clothes at the laundromat every sixth day. Janelle washes her clothes there every fifteenth day. If they both wash their clothes on the first of May, when will they both wash their clothes on the same day again?

   ____

Practice 8-5

Classifying Triangles and Quadrilaterals

Determine the best name for each quadrilateral. Explain your choice.

1. 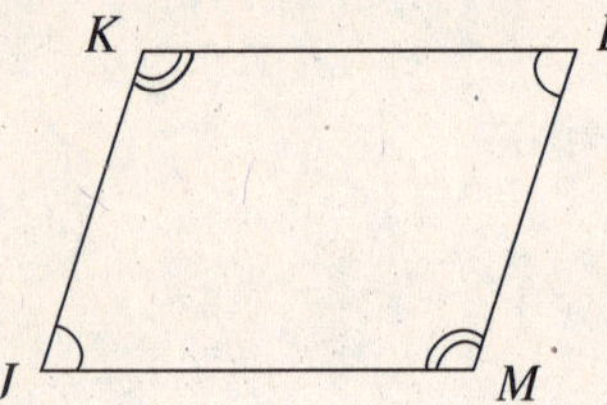

____

____

2. 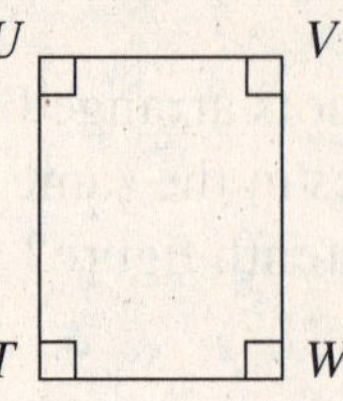

____

____

3. 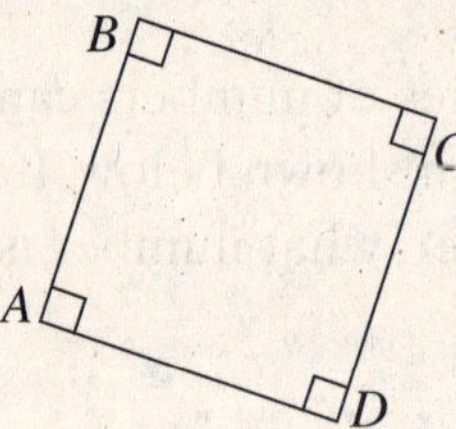

____

____

4. 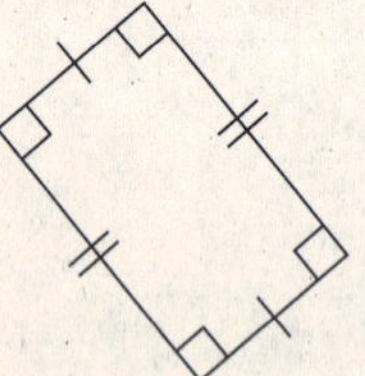

____

____

5. 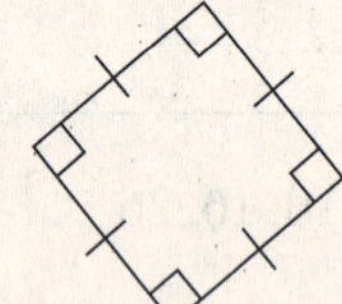

____

____

6. 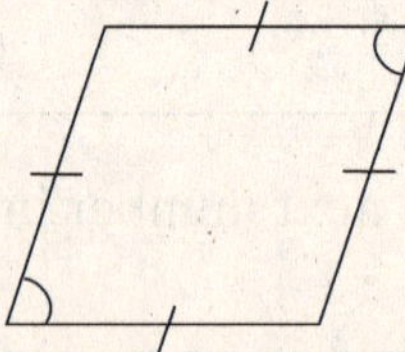

____

____

7. 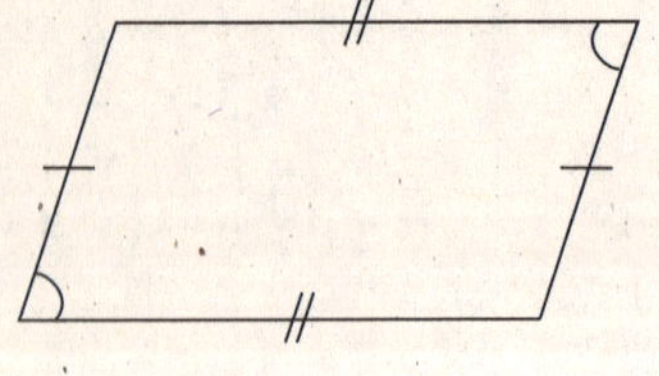

____

____

8. 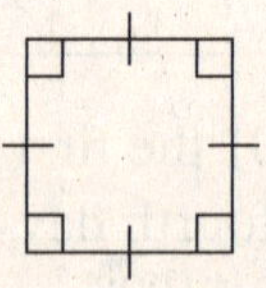

____

____

9. $\triangle ABC \cong \triangle CDA$

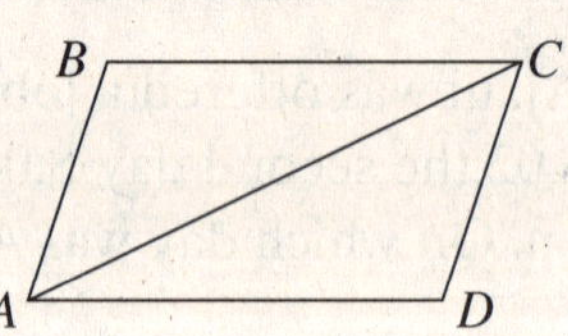

____

____

Classify each triangle by its sides and its angles. Explain your choice.

10. 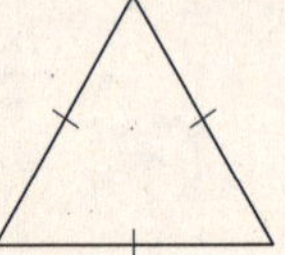

____

____

11. 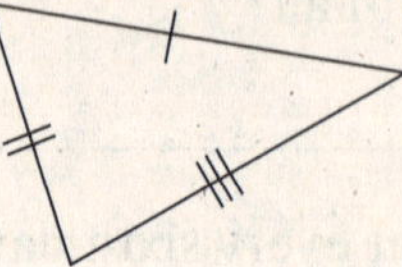

____

____

12. 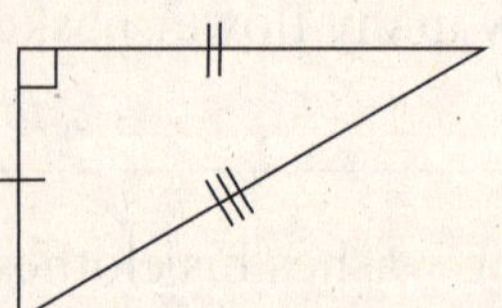

____

____

Practice 8-6

Angles and Polygons

Classify each polygon by the number of its sides.

1. 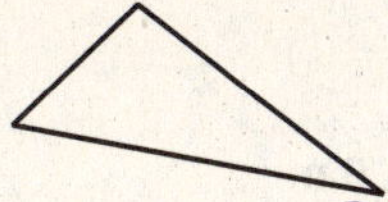 2. 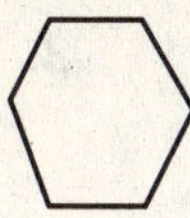 3. 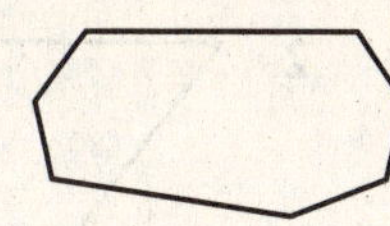 4. 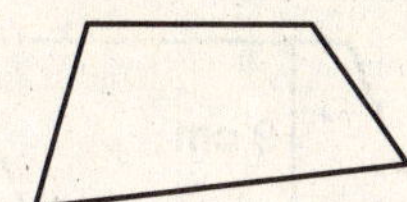

_______________ _______________ _______________

5. a polygon with 8 sides

6. a polygon with 10 sides

7. Find the measure of each angle of a regular hexagon.

8. The measures of four angles of a pentagon are 143°, 118°, 56°, and 97°. Find the measure of the missing angle.

9. What is the sum of the measures of the angles in a figure having 9 sides?

10. What is the sum of the measures of the angles of a figure having 11 sides?

11. Four of the angles of a hexagon measure 53°, 126°, 89°, and 117°. What is the sum of the measures of the other two angles?

12. Four of the angles of a heptagon measure 109°, 158°, 117°, and 89°. What is the sum of the measures of the other three angles?

13. Complete the chart for the total number of diagonals from all vertices in each polygon. The first three have been done for you.

Polygon	Number of Sides	Number of Diagonals
triangle	3	0
rectangle	4	2
pentagon	5	5
hexagon		
heptagon		
octagon		
nonagon		
decagon		

14. From the table you completed in Exercise 13, what pattern do you see? Explain.

____

____

Practice 8-7

Areas of Polygons

Find the area of each polygon.

1. 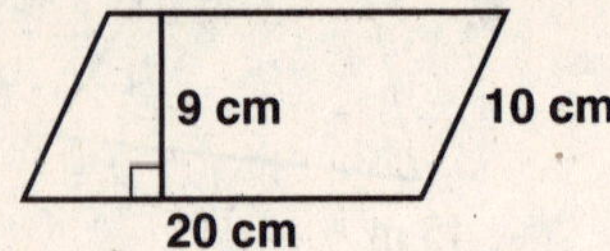

____

2. 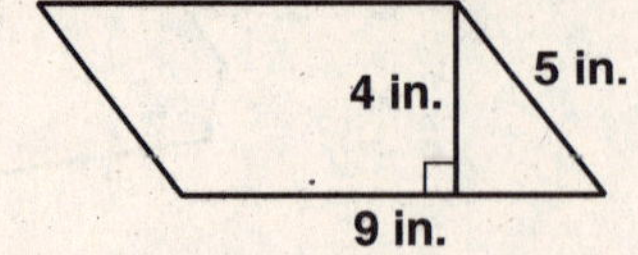

____

3. 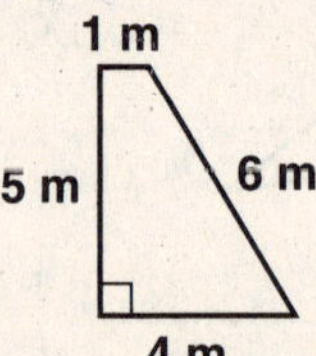

____

4. 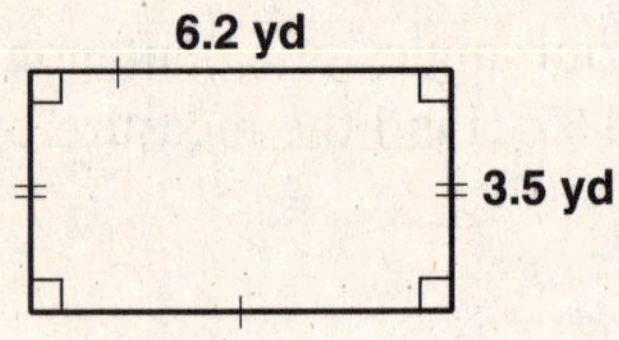

____

5. 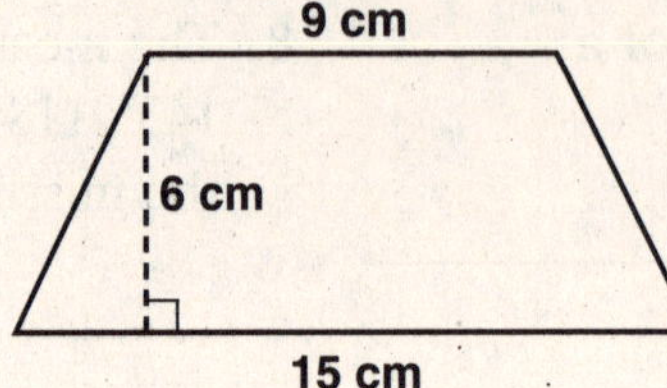

____

6. 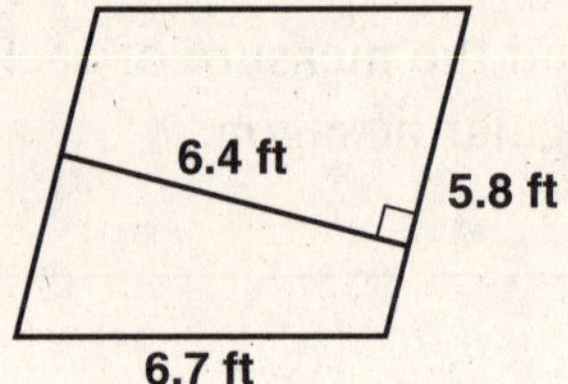

____

7. 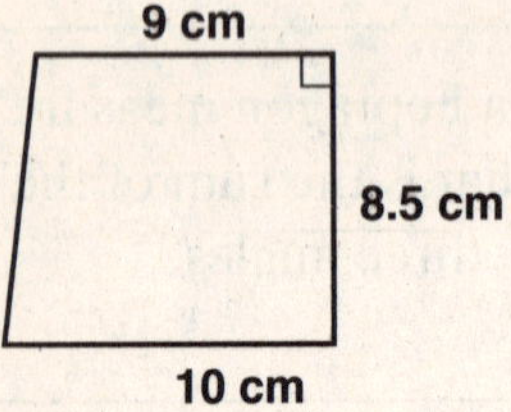

____

8. 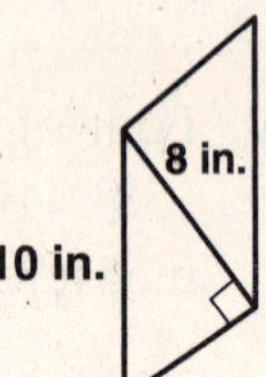

____

9. 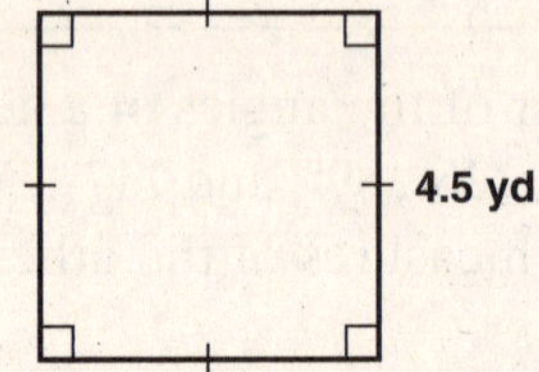

____

10. The area of a parallelogram is 221 yd². Its height is 13 yd. What is the length of its corresponding base?

____

11. The area of a parallelogram is 116 cm². Its base is 8 cm. What is the corresponding height?

____

Find the area of each triangle.

12. 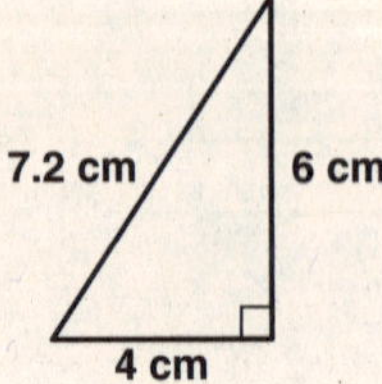

____

13. 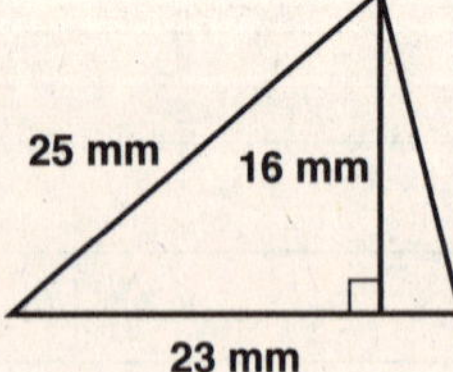

____

14. 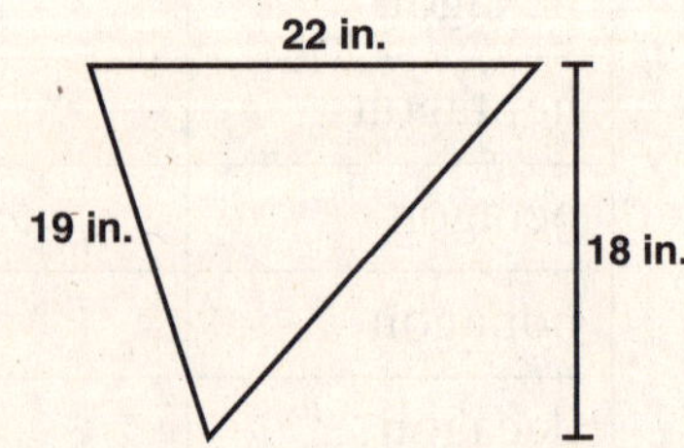

____

Practice 8-8

Circumferences and Areas of Circles

Find the circumference and area of each circle. Round to the nearest hundredth.

1. 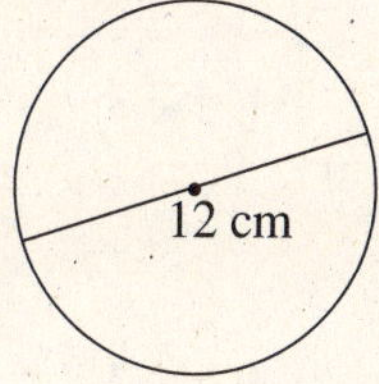

____

____

2. 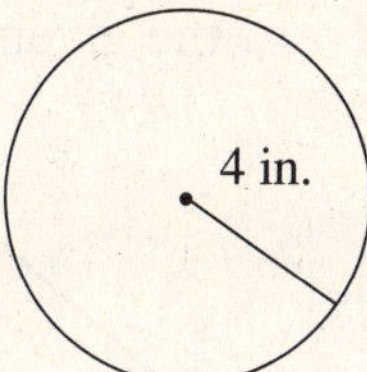

3. 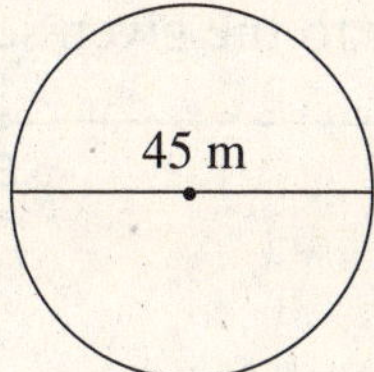

4. 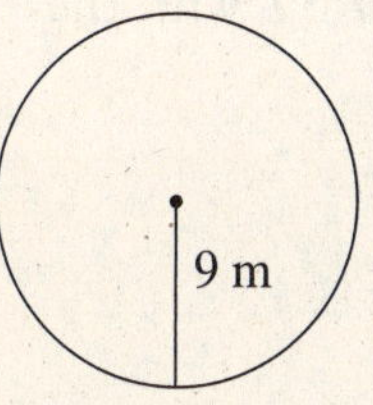

____

____

5. 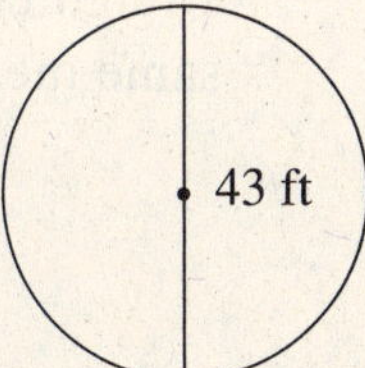

6. 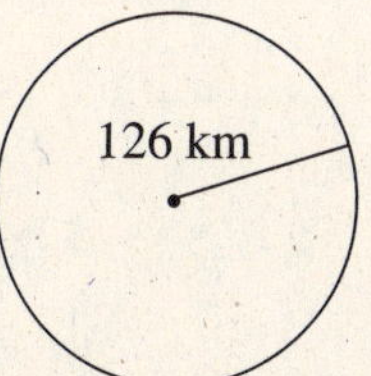

Find the circumference of a circle with the given diameter or radius. Use $\frac{22}{7}$ for π.

7. $d = 70$ cm

8. $r = 14$ cm

9. $d = 35$ in.

____

Find the radius and the diameter of a circle with the given circumference. Round to the nearest hundredth.

10. $C = 68$ cm

11. $C = 150$ m

12. $C = 218$ in.

____

13. Use the figure at the right. Find the area of the shaded region. Round your answer to the nearest hundredth.

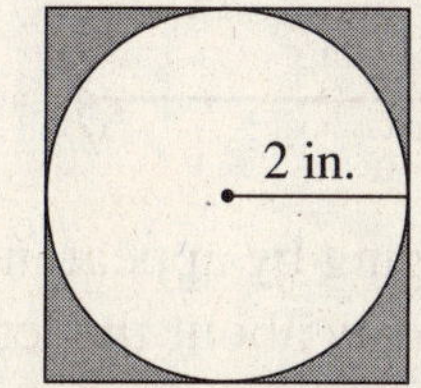

____

Practice 8-9

Constructions

Use a compass and straightedge to make each construction.

1. Construct segment $\overline{YZ}$ so that it is congruent to the given segment $\overline{AB}$.

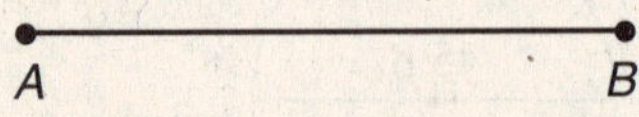

2. Construct $\angle PQR$ so that it is congruent to the given $\angle DEF$.

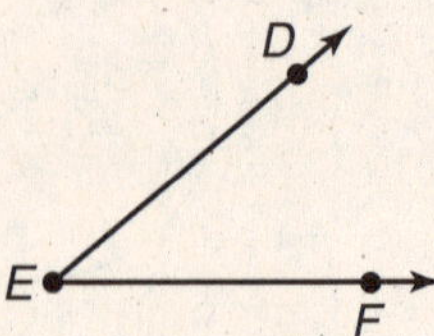

3. Draw an obtuse $\angle G$. Construct an angle congruent to $\angle G$.

4. Use a protractor to draw $\angle XYZ$ with $m\angle XYZ = 36°$. Then use a compass and straightedge to construct $\angle RST$ with the same measure.

5. Construct the perpendicular bisector of the given segment $\overline{JK}$.

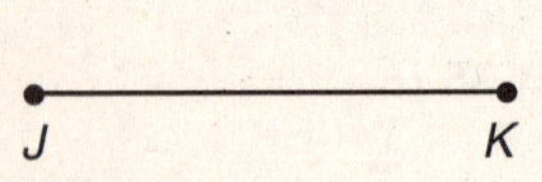

6. Construct the angle bisector of $\angle PRS$.

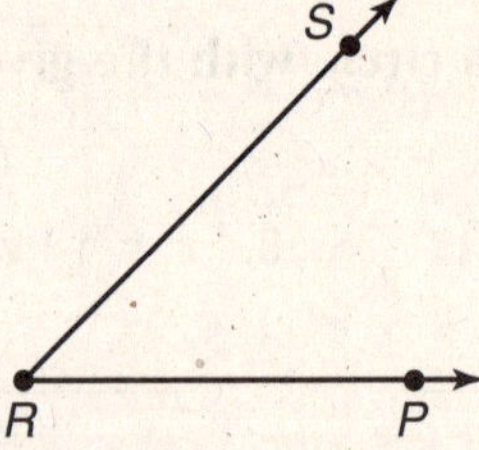

7. Use the figures below to complete triangle TUV. First, construct $\overline{TU}$ from the ray given with endpoint U. Make it congruent to $\overline{CD}$. Then draw $\overline{TV}$.

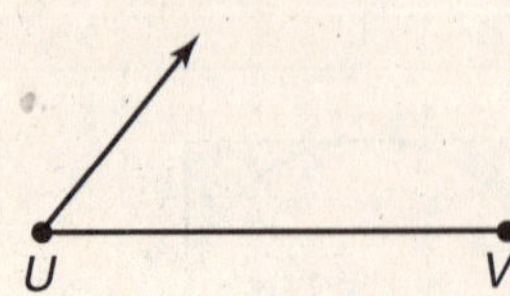

C   D

a. Judging by appearance, what might you say about the lengths TU and TV?

____

b. How could you use a compass to check your observation in part a?

____

____

____

Practice 9-1

Solids

For each figure, describe the base(s) of the figure, and name the figure.

1. 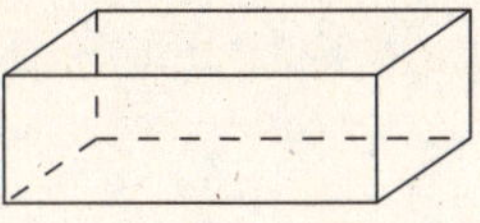

2. 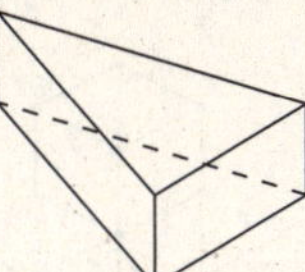

3. 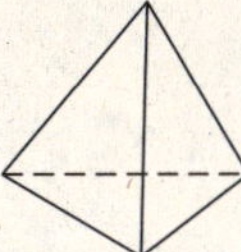

4. 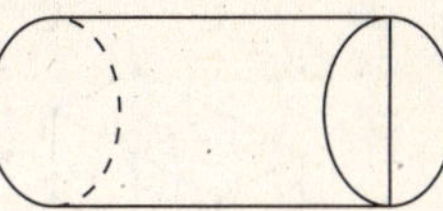

____

____

5. 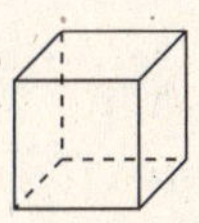

6. 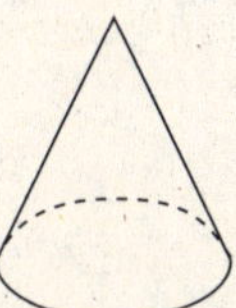

7. 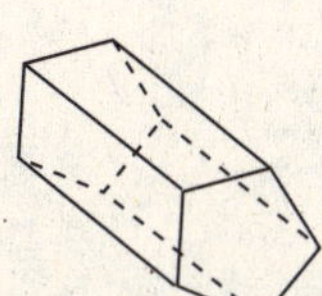

8. 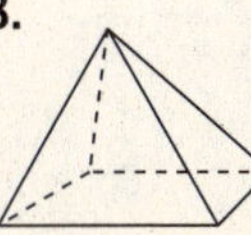

____

____

Name each solid according to its description.

9. bowling ball   **10.** VCR   **11.** soup can   **12.** funnel

____

Complete.

13. A _________________ has exactly two circular bases.

14. A hexagonal prism has _________________ faces.

15. A cube has _________________ edges.

16. A pentagonal pyramid has _________________ faces.

17. A pentagonal pyramid has _________________ edges.

18. A rectangular prism has _________________ vertices.

Name the figure described.

19. A space figure with six congruent square faces.

20. A space figure with parallel bases that are congruent, parallel circles.

____

21. On a sheet of graph paper, draw a rectangular prism.

Practice 9-2

Drawing Views of Three-Dimensional Figures

Draw a base plan for each set of stacked cubes.

1.

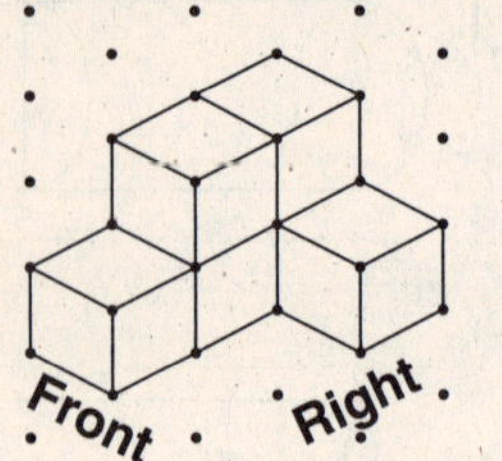

2.

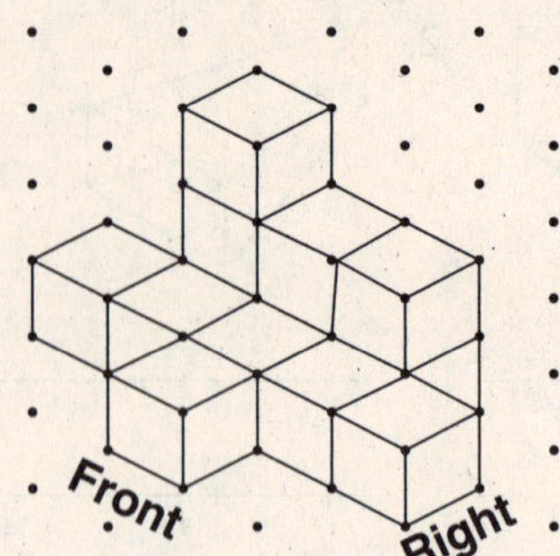

Draw the top, front, and right views of each figure.

3.

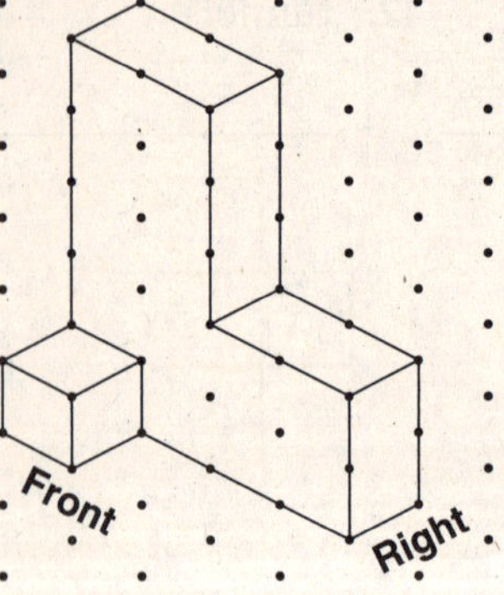

4.

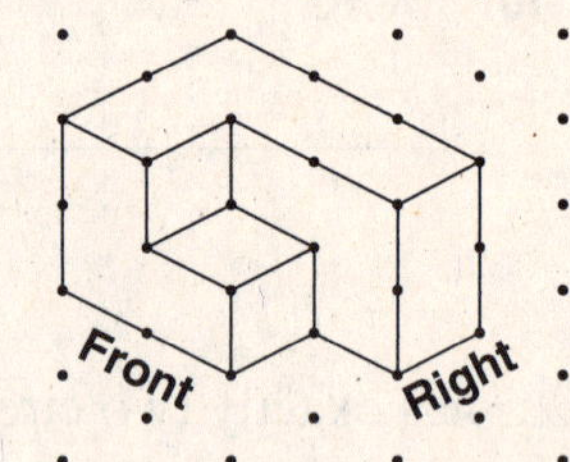

Practice 9-3

Nets and Three-Dimensional Figures

List the shapes that make up the net for each figure, and write the number of times each shape is used.

1. rectangular prism

____

____

2. pentagonal pyramid

____

____

3. cylinder

____

____

4. triangular pyramid

____

____

5. cone

____

____

6. hexagonal prism

____

____

7. Draw a net for a rectangular box that is 9 cm long, 5 cm wide, and 3 cm tall.

8. Draw a net for a cylinder whose height is 8 in. and whose radius is 3 in.

Identify the solid that each net forms.

9. 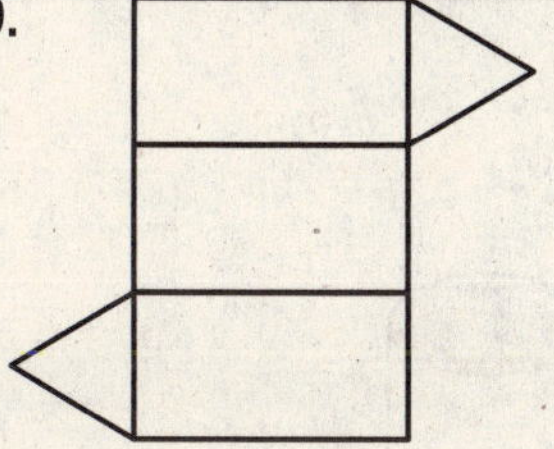

10. 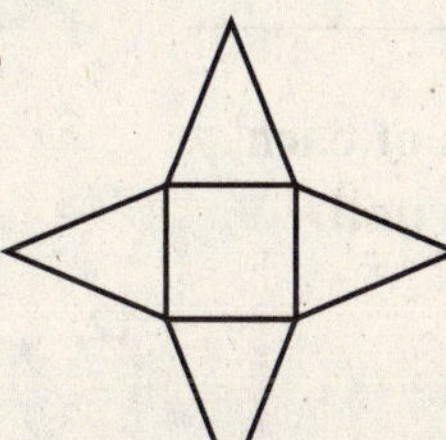

11. 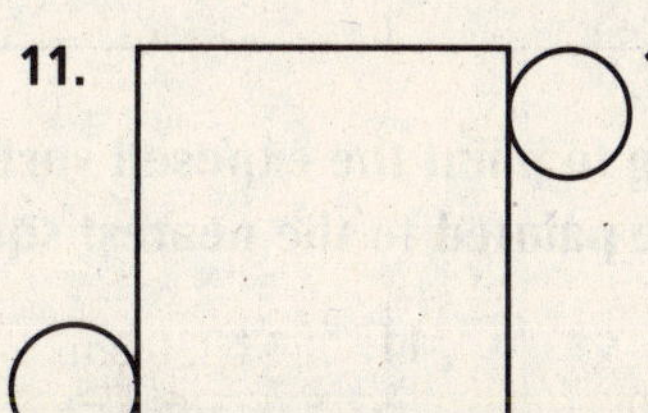

12. 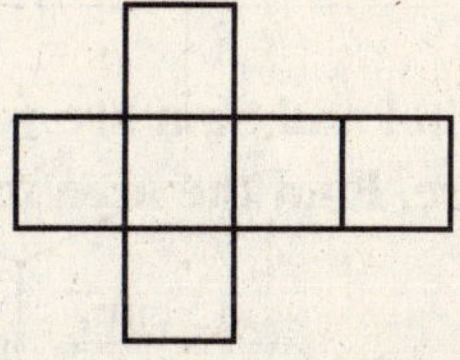

_______________________   _______________________

_______________________   _______________________

13. What three-dimensional figure can be made from this net?

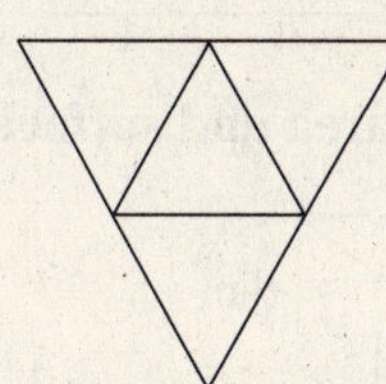

____

Practice 9-4

Surface Areas of Prisms and Cylinders

Use a net or a formula to find the surface area of each figure to the nearest square unit.

1. 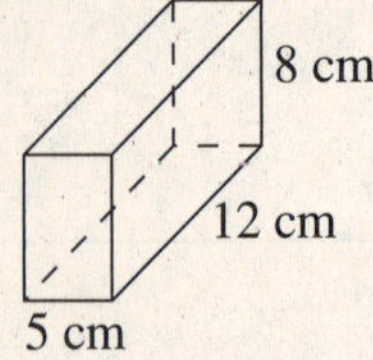

2. 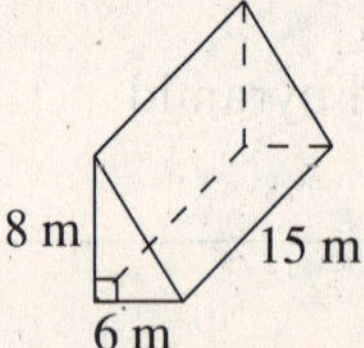

3. 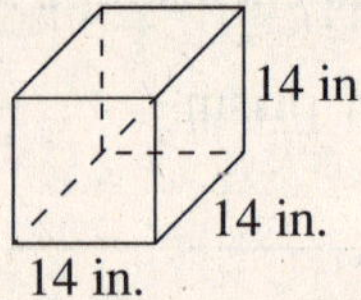

____

4. 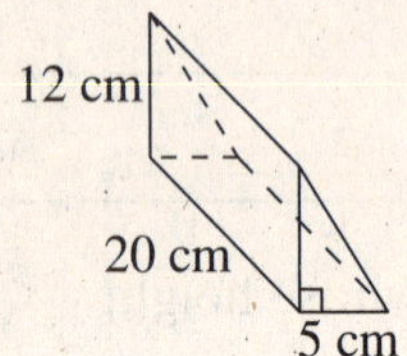

5. 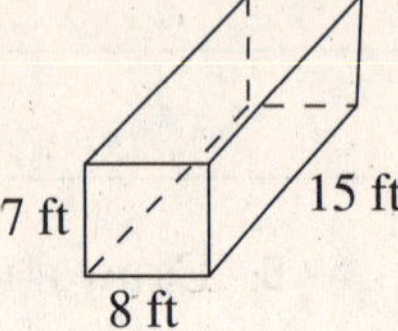

6. 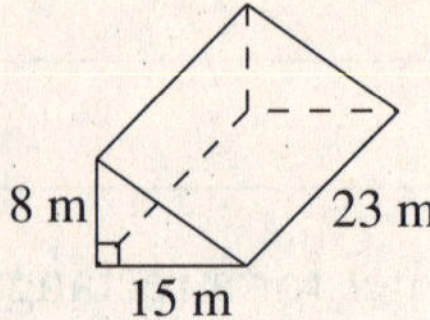

____

7. 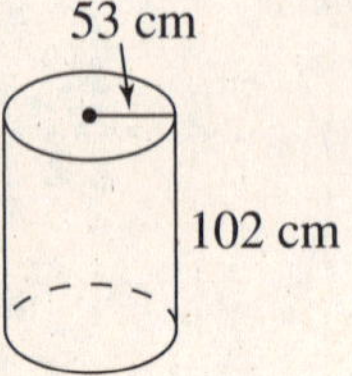

8. 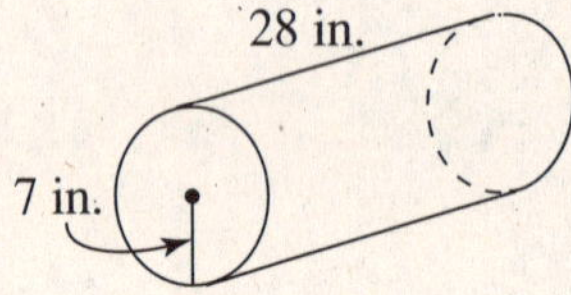

9. 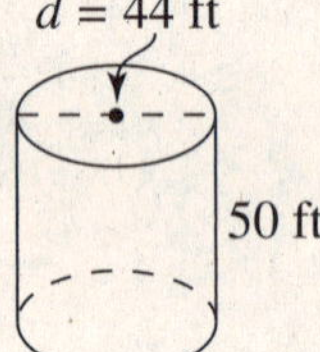

____

Rachel and Sam are going to paint the exposed surfaces of each figure. Find the area to be painted to the nearest square unit.

10. 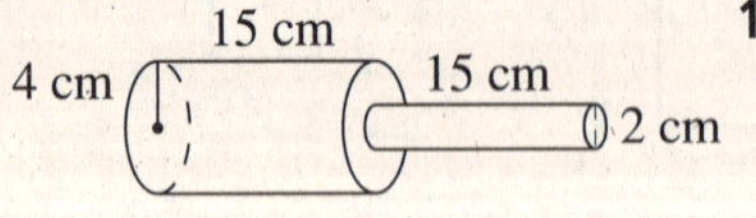

11. 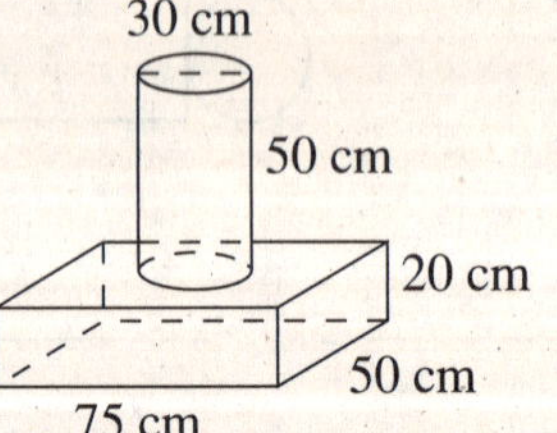

12. 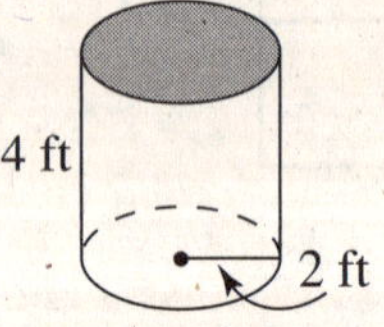

This cylinder does not have a top.

____

Find the lateral area and surface area of each figure. Round to the nearest square unit.

13. 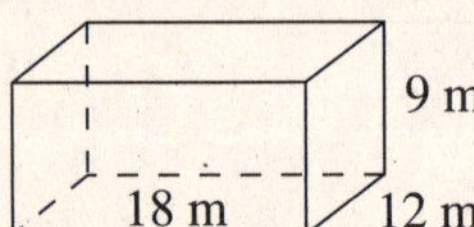

14. 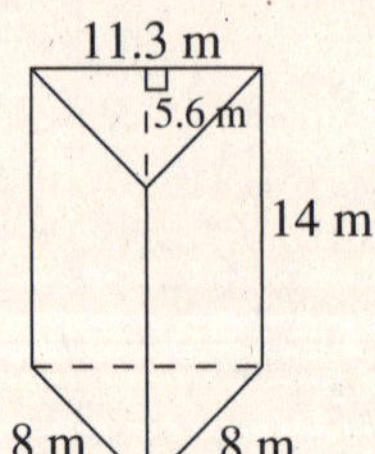

15. 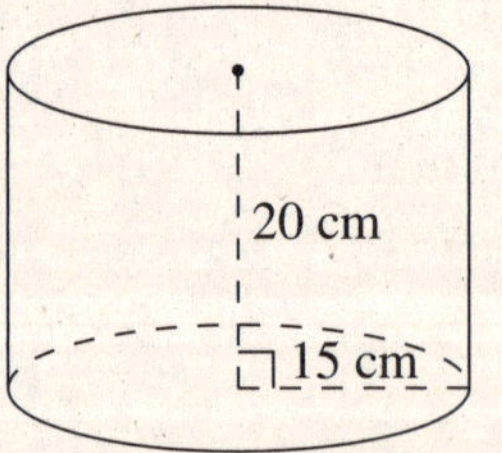

____

Practice 9-5

Surface Areas of Pyramids and Cones

Use a net to find the surface area of each square pyramid to the nearest square unit.

1. 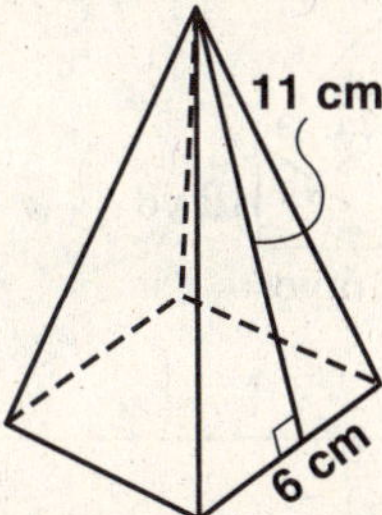

____

2. 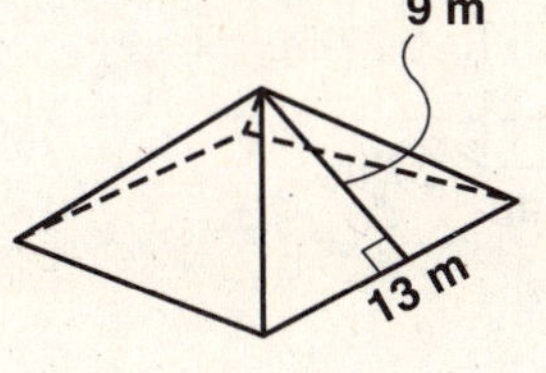

____

3. 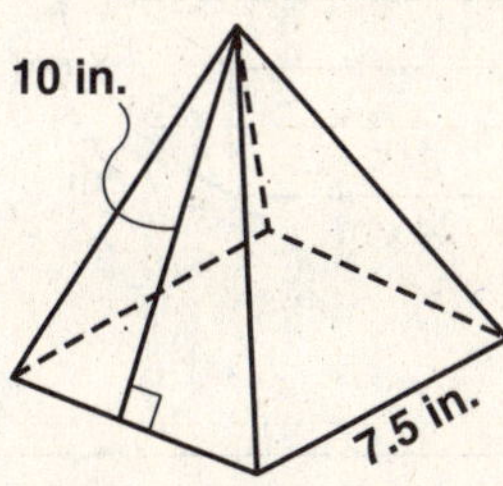

____

Find the lateral area of each pyramid to the nearest whole square unit.

4. 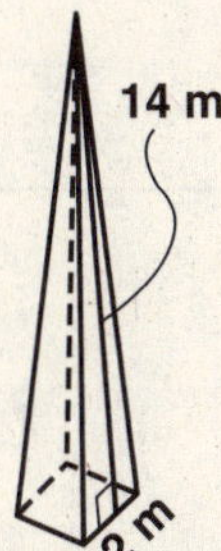

____

5. 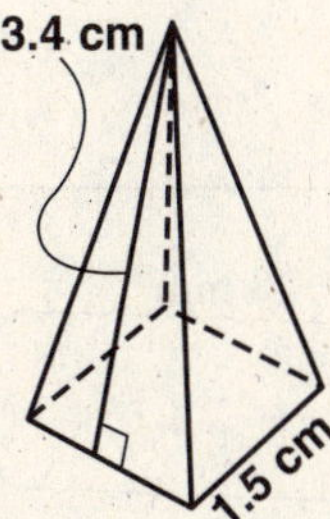

____

6. 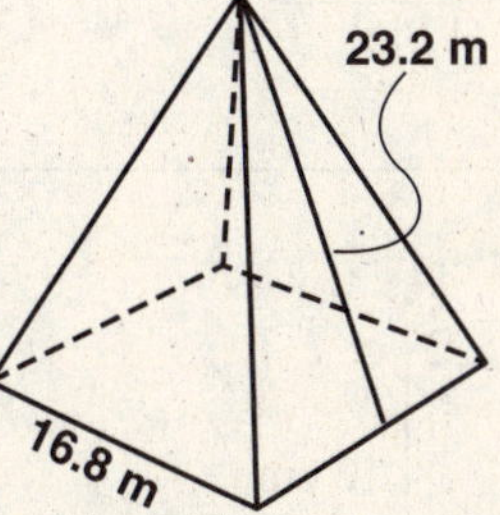

____

Find the surface area of each cone to the nearest square unit.

7. 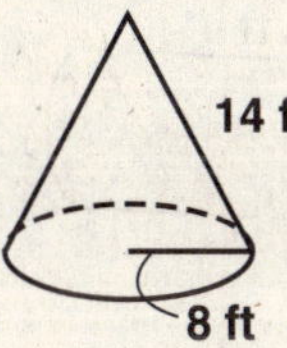

____

8. 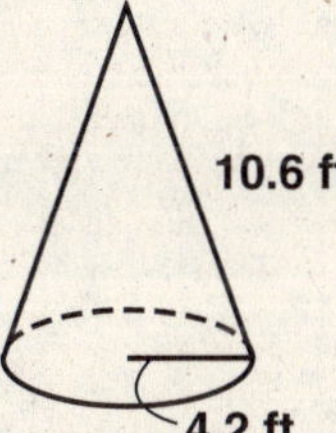

____

9. 

____

Find the lateral area of each cone to the nearest square unit.

10. 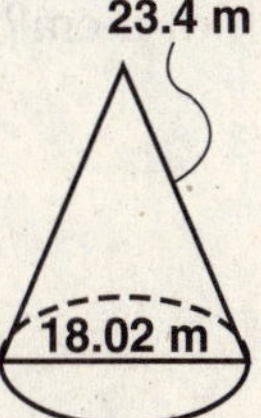

____

11. 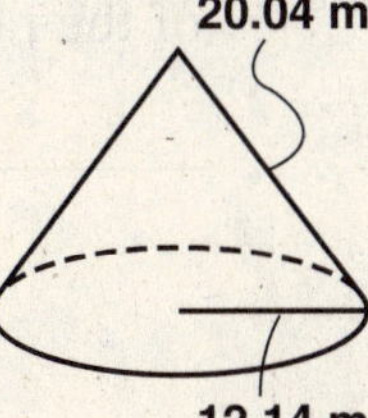

____

12. 

____

Practice 9-6

Volumes of Prisms and Cylinders

Find the volume of each solid to the nearest whole unit.

1.
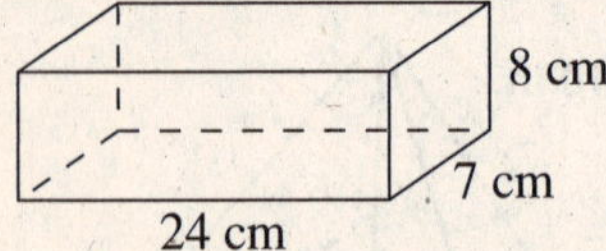

2.
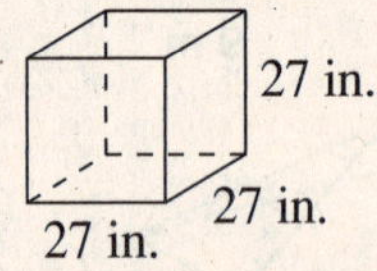

3.
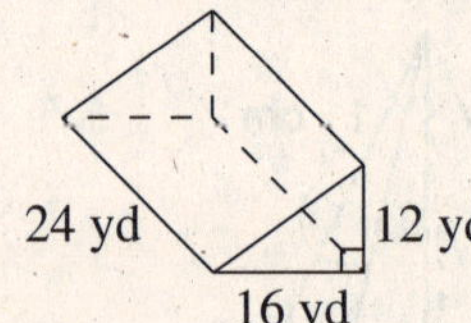

____

4.
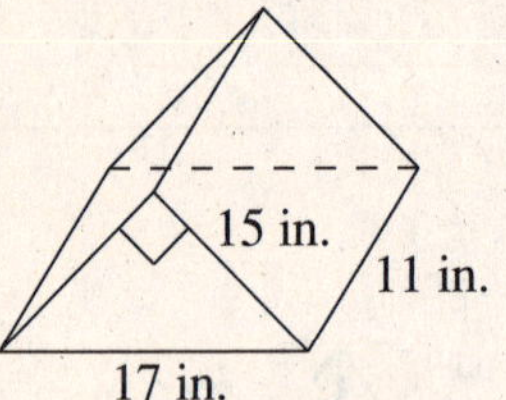

5.
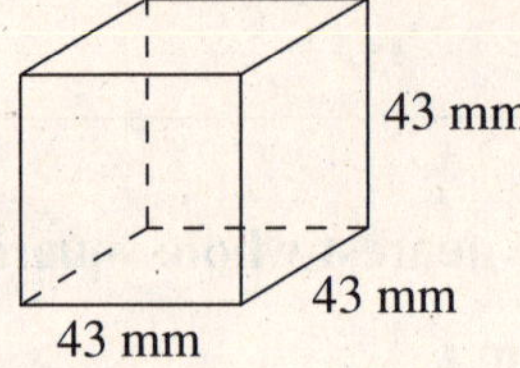

6.
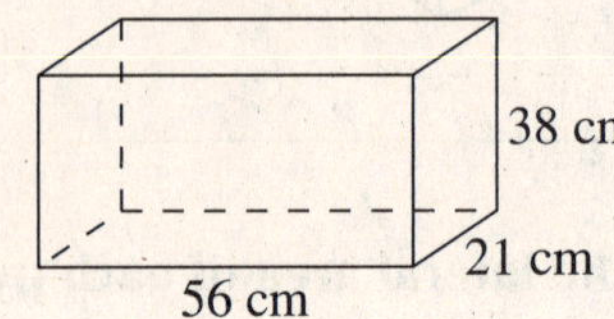

____

7.
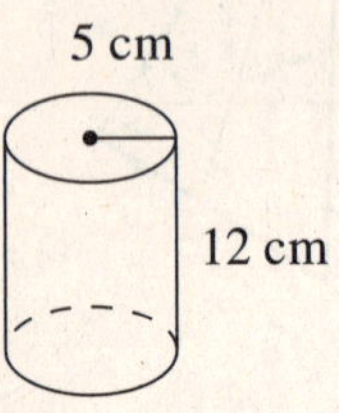

8.
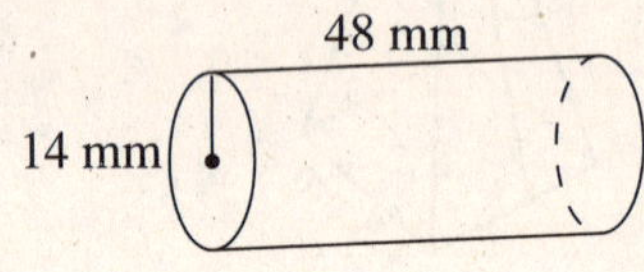

9.
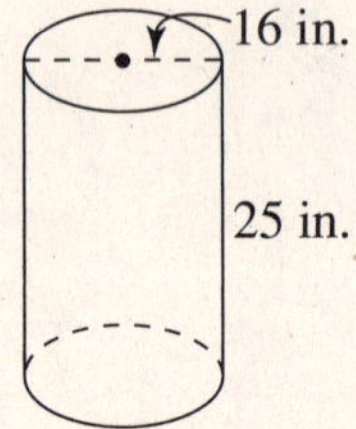

____

10.
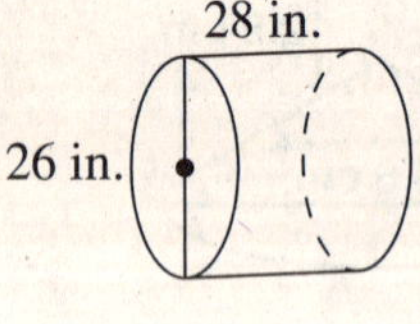

11.
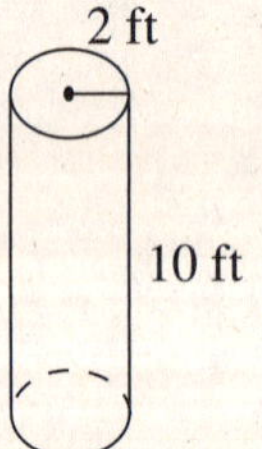

12.
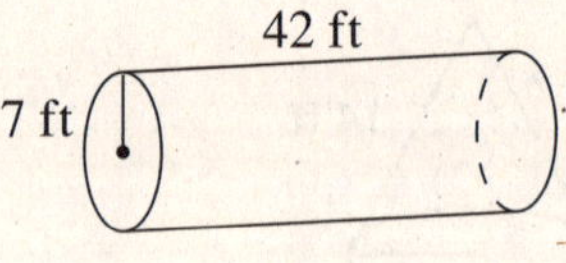

____

13. Suppose you want to buy concrete for a 36 ft by 24 ft by 9 in. patio. If concrete costs $55/yd^3, how much will the concrete for the patio cost?

14. A cylinder has a volume of about 500 cm^3 and a height of 10 cm. What is the length of the radius to the nearest tenth of a cm?

____

Practice 9-7

Volumes of Pyramids and Cones

Find the volume of each figure to the nearest cubic unit.

1. 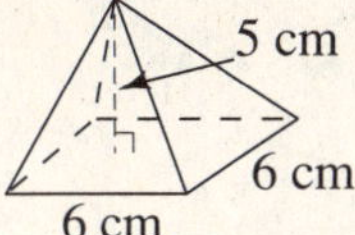

2. 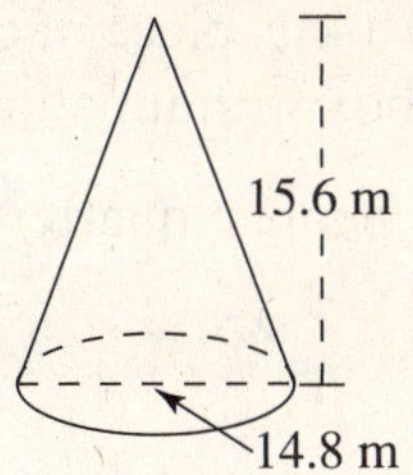

3. 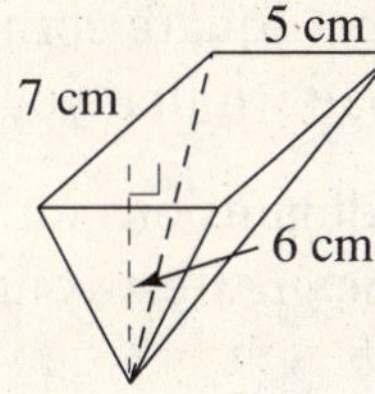

__________________________   __________________________   __________________________

4. 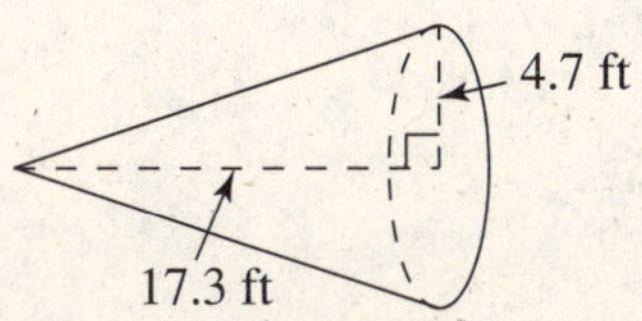

5. 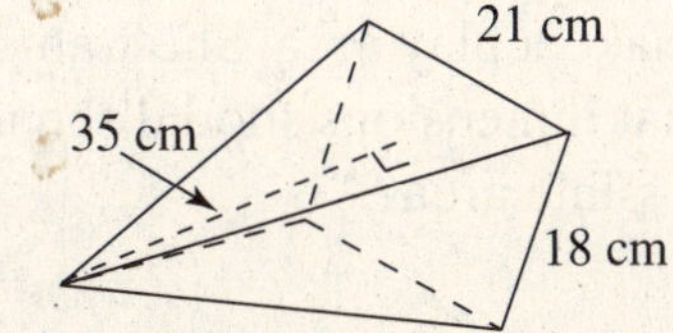

6. 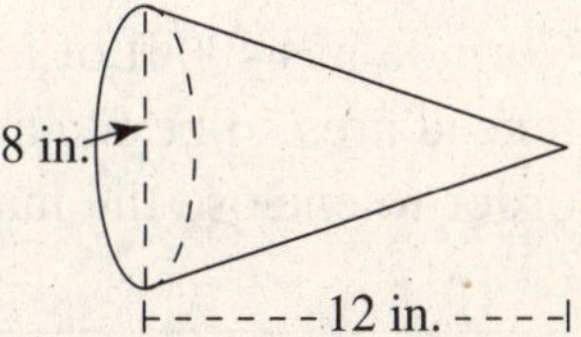

__________________________   __________________________   __________________________

Find the missing dimension for each three-dimensional figure to the nearest tenth, given the volume and other dimensions.

7. rectangular pyramid,
$l = 8$ m, $w = 4.6$ m, $V = 88$ m^3

8. cone, $r = 5$ in., $V = 487$ in.^{3}

__________________________   __________________________

9. square pyramid, $s = 14$ yd, $V = 489$ yd^3

10. square pyramid, $h = 8.9$ cm, $V = 56$ cm^3

__________________________   __________________________

11. cone, $h = 18$ cm, $V = 986$ cm^3

12. cone, $r = 5.5$ ft, $V = 592$ ft^3

__________________________   __________________________

13. Find the volume of a 4 ft by 2 ft by 3 ft rectangular prism with a cylindrical hole, radius 6 in., through the center.

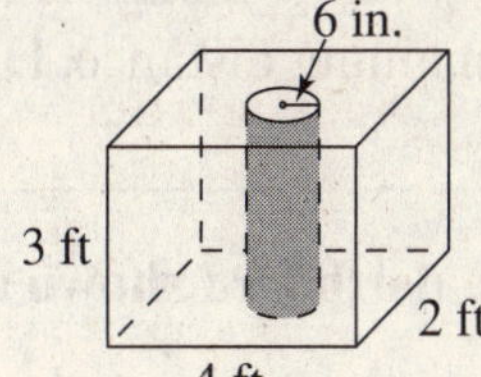

____

14. Margarite has a cylindrical tin of popcorn that is 18 in. tall and has a radius of 4 in. She wants to use the tin for something else and needs to empty the popcorn into a box. The box is 8 in. long, 8 in. wide, and 14 in. tall. Will the popcorn fit in the box? Explain.

____

____

Practice 9-8

Problem Solving: Draw a Diagram and Make a Table

Choose a strategy or a combination of strategies to solve each problem.

1. You can cut square corners off an 11 in. by 14 in. piece of cardboard to get a pattern that you could fold into a box without a top.

   a. What dimensions for the corners, to the nearest quarter-inch, will give the greatest volume?

   ____

   b. What is the greatest volume of the box to the nearest tenth?

   ____

2. Corinda has 400 ft of fencing to make a play area. She wants the fenced area to be rectangular. What dimensions should she use in order to enclose the maximum possible area?

   ____

3. A restaurant dining room measures 100 ft by 150 ft. The height of the room is 9 ft. If the occupancy guidelines recommend at least 150 ft³ per person, what is the maximum number of people that can be in the room?

   ____

4. Maurice lives at point A. The library is at point B. How many different routes can Maurice take from home to the library if he only goes to the right and down, never retracing his route?

   ____

5. The consecutive even integers from 2 to n are 2, 4, 6, ... , n. The square of the sum of the integers is 5,184. What is the value of n?

   ____

6. A bicyclist has 120 mi to cover on a trip. One day she bicycles 40% of the distance. The next day she cycles 60% of the remaining distance. How much further does she have to cycle?

   ____

Use the dartboard shown at the right.

7. Three darts are thrown at the target. If each dart lands on the target, how many *different* point totals are possible?

   ____

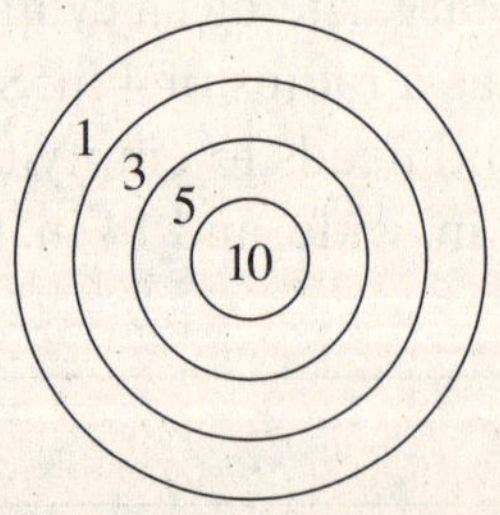

8. If 3 darts are thrown at the target and each dart lands on a different zone, find the maximum number of points scored.

   ____

Practice 9-9

Exploring Similar Solids

Complete the table for each prism.

	Original Size		Doubled Dimensions		
	Dimensions (m)	S.A. (m^2)	Dimensions (m)	S.A. (m^2)	New S.A. ÷ Old S.A.
1.	$2 \times 3 \times 4$				
2.	$5 \times 5 \times 9$				
3.	$7 \times 7 \times 7$				
4.	$8 \times 12 \times 15$				
5.	$15 \times 15 \times 20$				
6.	$32 \times 32 \times 32$				

7. What conclusion can you draw?

____

____

8. A rectangular prism is 8 cm by 10 cm by 15 cm. What are the volume and surface area of the prism?

____

9. In Exercise 8, if each dimension of the prism is halved, what are the new volume and surface area?

____

Use the triangular prism shown at the right for Exercises 10 and 11.

10. Find the volume and surface area.

____

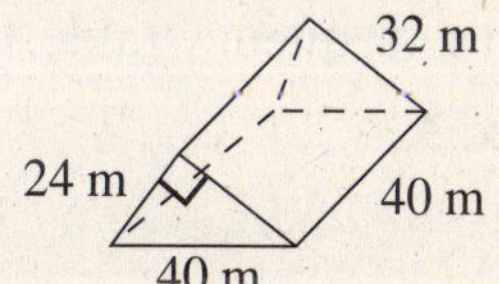

11. If each dimension of the prism is doubled, what are the new volume and surface areas?

____

12. A rectangular prism is 9 in. long, 15 in. wide, and 21 in. high. The length is halved. What happens to the volume?

____

13. A rectangular prism is 8 cm long, 24 cm wide, and 43 cm high. The length is doubled, and the width is tripled. What happens to the volume?

____

Practice 10-1

Displaying Frequency

Use the Olympic medal data at the right for Exercises 1–3.
Use the space below or a separate sheet of paper.

1. Make a frequency table. Do not use intervals.

2002 Winter Olympic Gold Medals	
Country	**Medals**
Germany	12
Norway	11
U.S.A.	10
Russia	6
Canada	6
France	4
Italy	4
Finland	4
Netherlands	3
Switzerland	3
Croatia	3
Austria	2
China	2
Korea	2
Australia	2

2. Draw a line plot.

3. Draw a histogram.

Use these ages of bike club members for Exercises 4 and 5. Use the
space below or a separate sheet of paper.

19   16   10   14   15   19   13   14   15   16   21   14   12   14   16   13   13

4. Using intervals, display the data in a frequency table.

   Ex. 3

5. Use the frequency table to draw a histogram.

   Ex. 4

   Ex. 5

Practice 10-2

Reading Graphs Critically

Use the graph below for Exercises 1–5.

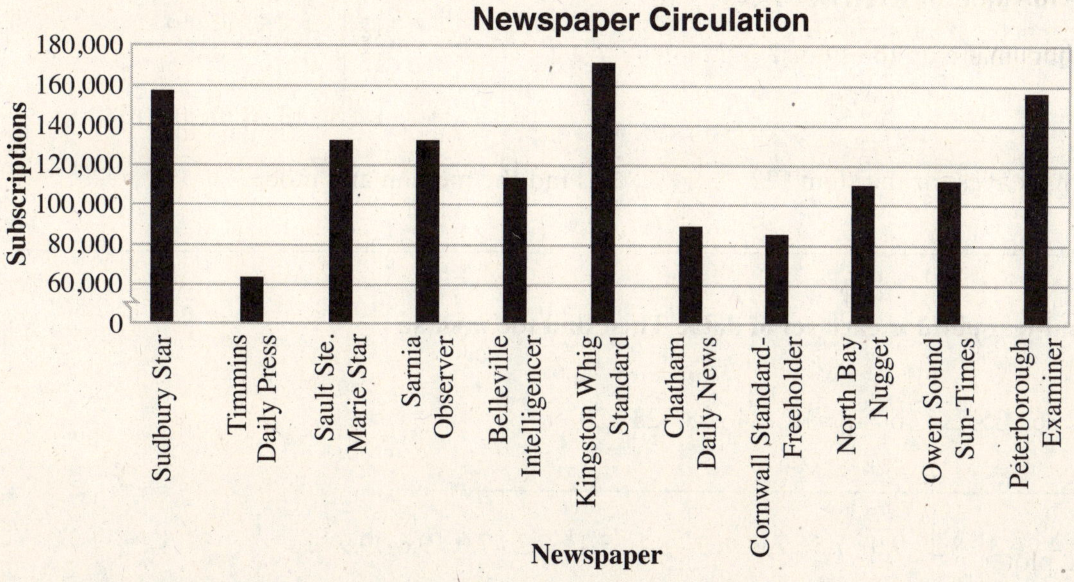

1. Which newspaper appears to have twice the circulation of
   The Cornwall Standard-Freeholder? ____________________

2. Which newspaper actually has about twice the circulation of
   The Cornwall Standard-Freeholder? ____________________

3. *Belleville Intelligencer* appears to have about how many times
   the circulation of *Chatham Daily News*? ____________________

4. Explain why the graph gives a misleading visual impression of
   the data.

   ____

   ____

5. Redraw the graph to give an accurate impression of the data.

Practice 10-3

Stem-and-Leaf Plots

The stem-and-leaf plot at the right shows the bowling scores for
20 bowlers. Use the plot for Exercises 1–3.

10	0 2 2 4 4 4
11	1 3 5 5 5 9
12	4 5 9 9
13	0 6 8 8

Key   13 | 8 means 138

1. What numbers make up the stems?

____

2. What are the leaves for the stem 12?

____

3. Find the median and mode.

____

**Make a stem-and-leaf plot for each set of data. Then find the median
and mode.**

4. 8 19 27 36 35 24 6 15 16 24 38 23 20

____

5. 8.6 9.1 7.4 6.3 8.2 9.0 7.5 7.9 6.3 8.1 7.1 8.2 7.0 9.6 9.9

____

6. 436 521 470 586 692 634 417 675 526 719 817

____

7. 17.9 20.4 18.6 19.5 17.6 18.5 17.4 18.5 19.4

____

**The back-to-back stem-and-leaf plot at the right shows the high and
low temperatures for a week in a certain city. Use this plot for
Exercises 8–10.**

Low		High
8 7	5	
4 3	6	5 9 9
2 1 0	7	2 5 6
	8	0

63 ← 3 | 6 | 5 → 65

8. Find the mean for the high temperatures.

____

9. Find the median for the low temperatures.

____

10. Find the mode for the high temperatures.

____

11. Make a back-to-back stem-and-leaf plot for the following data.
Then find the median and mode.

Set A: 75 82 79 80 75 76 83 74 75 86 80 71 75 _______________

Set B: 71 73 75 80 79 80 74 80 74 79 76 80 81 _______________

Practice 10-4

Box-and-Whisker Plots

Use the box-and-whisker plot to find each value.

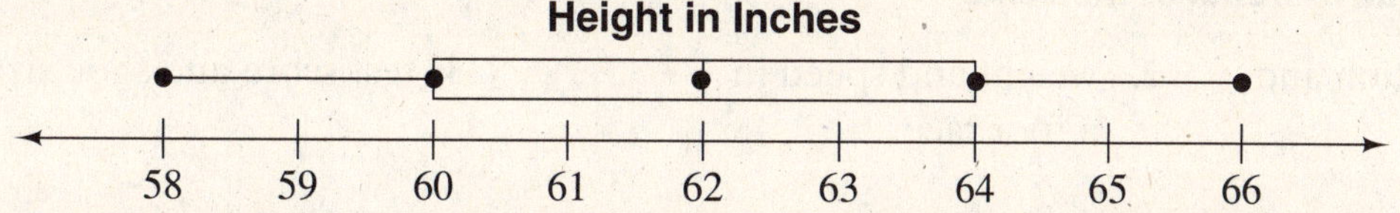

1. the median height _______________________
2. the lower quartile _______________________

3. the upper quartile _______________________
4. the greatest height _______________________

5. the shortest height _______________________
6. the range of heights _______________________

Make a box-and-whisker plot for each set of data.

7. 8   10   11   7   12   6   10   5   9   7   10

8. 20   21   25   18   25   15   27   26   24   23   20   20

9.

Cargo Airlines in the U.S. (1991)	
Airline	**Freight ton-miles (1,000,000s)**
Federal Express	3,622
Northwest	1,684
United	1,214
American	884
Delta	668
Continental	564
Pan American	377
Trans World	369
United Parcel Service	210

10.

Immigration to the U.S. (1981–1990)	
Country	**Number (1,000s)**
Mexico	1,656
Philippines	549
China	347
Korea	334
Vietnam	281
Dominican Republic	252
India	251
El Salvador	214
Jamaica	208
United Kingdom	159

Practice 10-5

Making Predictions from Scatter Plots

Tell whether a scatter plot made for each set of data would describe a positive trend, a negative trend, or no trend.

1. amount of education and annual salary

____

2. weight and speed in a foot race

____

3. test score and shoe size

____

4. Make a scatter plot showing the number of homeowners on one axis and vacation homeowners on the other axis. If there is a trend, draw a trend line.

Residents of Maintown		
Year	Homeowners	Vacation Homeowners
1997–98	2,050	973
1996–97	1,987	967
1995–96	1,948	1,041
1994–95	1,897	1,043
1993–94	1,862	1,125
1992–93	1,832	1,126

5. Make a scatter plot for the data. If there is a trend, draw a trend line.

Arm Span vs. Height		
Person #	Arm Span	Height
1	156	162
2	157	160
3	159	162
4	160	155
5	161	160
6	161	162
7	162	170
8	165	166
9	170	170
10	170	167
11	173	185
12	173	176

6. Wynetta found the graph shown at the right. The title of the graph was missing. What could the graph be describing?

____

____

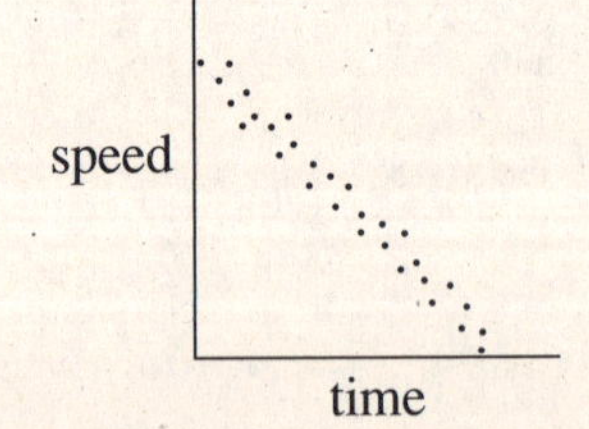

Practice 10-6

Circle Graphs

Use the circle graph for Exercises 1–2.

1. From which group are about $\frac{1}{3}$ of used cars purchased?

   ____

2. If 49,778 people bought used cars one month, estimate how many bought them from a dealership.

   ____

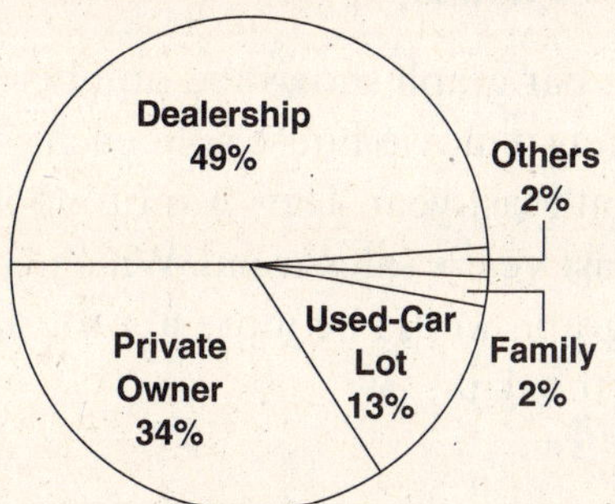

Make a circle graph for each set of data.

3.

Activity	Percent of Day
Sleep	25%
School	25%
Job	17%
Entertainment	17%
Meals	8%
Homework	8%

4.

Favorite Pet	Percent
Dogs	30%
Cats	25%
Fish	12%
Birds	11%
Other	22%

5.

Type of Milk	Percent
Skim	27%
Lowfat	37%
Whole	36%

6.

Activity	Percent
Visiting w/Friends	26%
Talk on Phone	26%
Play Sports	19%
Earn Money	19%
Use Computers	10%

Practice 10-7

**Use the graph to the right for
Exercises 1 and 2.**

1. The bar graph shows the number of
   tickets a movie house sold each
   month last year. They want to look
   at last year's sales trend. Which type
   of graph would be more appropriate
   for the data?

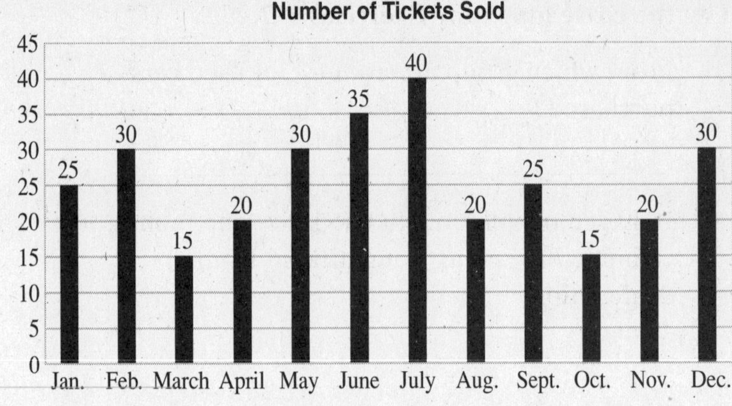

   ____

2. Draw the graph.

**Decide which type of graph would be the most appropriate for the
data. Explain your choice.**

3. sizes of U.S. farms from 1950 to 2000

   ____

4. lengths of rivers

   ____

5. height versus weight of students in a class

   ____

6. the way a family budgets its income

   ____

Practice 10-8

Draw a Diagram and Use Logical Reasoning

Solve each problem using logical reasoning to organize the information in a diagram.

1. Place the factors of 32 and 24 in a Venn diagram. What are common factors of 32 and 24? What is the greatest common factor?

Factors
32: 1, 2, 4, 8, 16, 32
24: 1, 2, 3, 4, 6, 8, 12, 24

2. A favorite subject poll of 30 students shows that 18 like Math, 9 like History, and 10 like English. Three students like all three subjects, 3 like Math and History, 4 like Math and English, and 3 like only English. How many students did not like any class?

3. Twenty-six students were asked if they have a job or are in a club. Eighteen students have a job and 15 are in a club. Four students do neither. Place the information in a Venn Diagram. How many students have a job and are in a club?

4. A survey on favorite kinds of books shows that 9 people like mysteries, 10 like adventure stories, and 8 enjoy biographies. Three of the people read only mysteries and adventure stories, 4 read only adventure stories and biographies, 4 read only mysteries and 2 read all three kinds of books. How many people were surveyed?

Choose a strategy or a combination of strategies to solve each problem.

5. Maria plans to donate $3 in January, $4 in February, $6 in March, and $9 in April. If she continues this pattern, how much money will she donate in December?

6. Elena is building a fence around her rabbit hutch. She plans to put 8 posts along each side. The diameter of each post is 6 inches. How many posts will there be?

7. Alicia, Benito, Claudio, and Donna are musicians. One plays the clarinet, one plays guitar, one is a pianist, and one sings. Alicia and Claudio saw the pianist perform. Benito and Claudio have heard the guitar player. The singer sang a song to Alicia and Donna. Bentio plays the clarinet. Who is the singer?

8. Laura is doing a picture puzzle with 520 pieces. When she has placed 4 times as many puzzle pieces as she has already placed, she will have 184 pieces left. How many puzzle pieces has Laura placed?

Practice 11-1

Counting Outcomes

Draw a tree diagram to show all possibilities.

1. Today, the school's cafeteria is offering a choice of pizza or spaghetti. You can get milk or juice to drink. For dessert you can get pudding or an apple. You must take one of each choice.

2. A clothing store sells shirts in three sizes: small, medium, and large. The shirts come with buttons or with snaps. The colors available are blue or beige.

Use the counting principle for Exercises 3–8.

3. A dinner menu at a restaurant offers 2 kinds of appetizers, 11 main courses, and 8 desserts. How many combinations of dinners are available?

   ____

4. A school assigns each student a 3-digit code number. How many possible 3-digit codes are there? What could cause the school to change to a 4-digit system?

   ____

   ____

5. A dress pattern offers two styles of skirts, three styles of sleeves, and four different collars. How many different types of dresses are available from one pattern?

   ____

6. In a class of 250 eighth graders, 14 are running for president, 12 are running for vice president, 9 are running for secretary, and 13 are running for treasurer. How many different results are possible for the class election?

   ____

7. A home alarm system has a 3-digit code that can be used to deactivate the system. If the homeowner forgets the code, how many different codes might the homeowner have to try?

   ____

8. A 4-letter password is required to enter a computer file. How many passwords are possible if no letter is repeated and nonsense words are allowed?

   ____

Practice 11-2

Permutations

Simplify each expression.

1. $6!$

2. $12!$

3. $9!$

4. $\dfrac{8!}{5!}$

5. $\dfrac{12!}{3!}$

6. $_9P_5$

7. $_8P_2$

8. $_{10}P_8$

9. $_5P_5$

10. $_{15}P_6$

Use the counting principle to find the number of permutations.

11. In how many ways can all the letters of the word WORK be arranged? _______________

12. In how many ways can you arrange seven friends in a row for a photo? _______________

13. A disk jockey can play eight songs in one time slot. In how many different orders can the eight songs be played?

14. Melody has nine bowling trophies to arrange in a horizontal line on a shelf. How many arrangements are possible?

15. At a track meet, 42 students entered the 100-m race. In how many ways can first, second, and third places be awarded?

16. In how many ways can a president, a vice president, and a treasurer be chosen from a group of 15 people running for office?

17. A car dealer has 38 used cars to sell. Each day two cars are chosen for advertising specials. One car appears in a television commercial and the other appears in a newspaper advertisement. In how many ways can the two cars be chosen?

18. A bicycle rack outside a classroom has room for six bicycles. In the class, 10 students sometimes ride their bicycles to school. How many different arrangements of bicycles are possible for any given day?

19. A certain type of luggage has room for three initials. How many different 3-letter arrangements of letters with no repetition of the same letter are possible?

20. A roller coaster has room for 10 people. The people sit single file, one after the other. How many different arrangements are possible for 10 passengers on the roller coaster?

Practice 11-3 Combindations

Combinations

Simplify each expression.

1. $_9C_1$ _________   **2.** $_8C_4$ _________   **3.** $_{11}C_4$ _________   **4.** $_{11}C_7$ _________

5. $_4C_4$ _________   **6.** $_9C_3$ _________   **7.** $_{12}C_6$ _________   **8.** $_8C_2$ _________

9. 3 videos from 10   **10.** 2 letters from   **11.** 4 books from 8   **12.** 5 people from 7

_________   LOVE _________   _________   _________

Solve.

13. Ten students from a class have volunteered to be on a committee to organize a dance. In how many ways can six be chosen for the committee?

____

14. Twenty-three people try out for extra parts in a play. In how many ways can eight people be chosen to be extras?

____

15. A team of nine players is to be chosen from 15 available players. In how many ways can this be done?

____

16. In a talent show, five semi-finalists are chosen from 46 entries. In how many ways can the semi-finalists be chosen?

____

17. At a party there are 12 people present. The host requests that each person present shakes hands exactly once with every other person. How many handshakes are necessary?

____

18. In math class there are 24 students. The teacher picks 4 students to serve on the bulletin board committee. How many different committees of 4 are possible?

____

19. Five friends, Billi, Joe, Eduardo, Mari, and Xavier, want one photograph taken of each possible pair of friends. Use B, J, E, M, and X, and list all of the pairs that need to be photographed.

____

20. A team of 3 people is chosen from 8 available players. Describe the number of possible teams using combination notation.

____

Practice 11-4

Theoretical and Experimental Probability

A dart is thrown at the game board shown. Notice that the diameters are at right angles and the slices that are congruent. Find each probability.

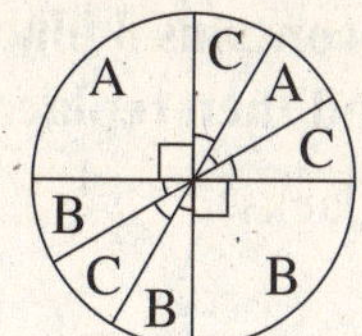

1. $P(A)$ _______

2. $P(B)$ _______

3. $P(C)$ _______

4. $P(\text{not } A)$ _______

5. $P(\text{not } B)$ _______

6. $P(\text{not } C)$ _______

The odds in favor of winning a game are 5 to 9.

7. Find the probability of winning the game. _______

8. Find the probability of *not* winning the game. _______

A box of marbles contains 10 red, 12 blue, 15 yellow, and 8 green marbles. A marble is drawn at random. Find each probability.

9. $P(\text{red})$ _______

10. $P(\text{blue})$ _______

11. $P(\text{yellow})$ _______

12. $P(\text{green})$ _______

13. What are the odds in favor of picking a blue marble?

____

14. What are the odds in favor of picking a green marble?

____

15. What is the probability of picking a marble that is not yellow?

____

16. What is the probability of picking a marble that is not red?

____

Solve.

17. a. You buy a ticket for the weekly drawing by a community charity. Last week you bought one ticket. Find the probability and odds of your winning if 1,200 tickets were bought that week.

____

b. Find the probability and odds of your winning if you bought three tickets and there were 1,200 tickets bought that week.

____

18. A bakery's bread-display case contains wheat and rye bread. If you randomly pick a slice of bread, $P(\text{wheat}) = 0.45$. Find $P(\text{rye})$. If there are 200 slices of bread, how many slices of wheat bread are in the display case?

____

Practice 11-5

Independent and Dependent Events

A drawer contains 3 black and 2 white socks. A sock is drawn at random and then replaced. Find each probability.

1. P(2 blacks)   **2.** P(black and white)   **3.** P(white and black)   **4.** P(2 whites)

___________   ___________   ___________   ___________

Each letter from the word MASSACHUSETTS is written on a separate slip of paper. The 13 slips of paper are placed in a sack and two slips are drawn at random. The first pick is not replaced.

5. Find the probability that the first letter is M and the second letter is S. ___________

6. Find the probability that the first letter is S and the second letter is A. ___________

7. Find the probability that the first letter is S and the second letter is also S. ___________

Solve.

8. On a TV game show, you can win a car by drawing a 1 and a 15 from a stack of cards numbered 1–15. The first card is not replaced. What is your probability of winning?

9. You roll a number cube eight times, and each time you roll a 4. What is the theoretical probability that on the ninth roll, you will roll a 6? Is rolling a 6 dependent or independent of rolling a 4 eight times?

___________   ___________________

10. Two letters of the alphabet are chosen randomly without replacement. Find each probability.

   a. P(both vowels) ___________   **b.** P(both consonants) ___________

11. There are 4 brown shoes and 10 black shoes on the floor. Your puppy carries away two shoes and puts one shoe in the trash can and one shoe in the laundry basket.

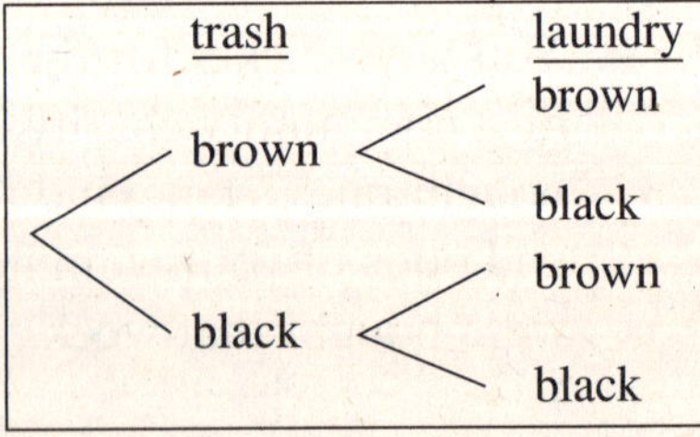

   a. Complete the tree diagram to show the probability of each outcome.

   b. What is the probability that there will be a brown shoe in both the trash and the laundry basket?

____

12. Use the data at the right to find P(right-handed female and left-handed male) if two people are chosen at random.

	Male	Female
Right-handed	86	83
Left-handed	14	17
Total	100	100

____

Practice 11-6

Problem Solving: Make an Organized List and Simulate a Problem

Solve by making an organized list or by simulating the problem.

1. The probability of a newborn puppy being either a male or female is $\frac{1}{2}$. What is the probability that a litter of 4 puppies contains 3 females?

   ____

2. In a mixed-badminton tournament, each team consists of one boy and one girl. Three boys and three girls signed up for the tournament. How many different badminton games can be played with different mixed-doubles teams?

   ____

The Coast Guard reports that the probability for calm water each day for the next few days is 50%. You begin a three-day sailing trip.

3. Simulate the situation to find the probability of three days of calm water in a row.

   ____

4. Simulate the situation to find the probability of only two days of calm water out of the three.

   ____

5. Simulate the situation to find the probability of only one day of calm water out of the three.

   ____

6. Simulate the situation to find the probability of no calm water for any of the three days.

   ____

A soccer player scores a goal on about 1 out of every 6 shots.

7. Explain how you could use a number cube to simulate the player's scoring average.

   ____

8. Use your simulation to find the probability of the player making 4 out of 5 of her next attempts.

   ____

Practice 11-7

Conducting a Survey

In a mall, 2,146 shoppers (age 16 and older) were asked, "How often do you eat at a restaurant in the mall?" Here is how they responded.

1. What population does the sample represent?

   ____

   ____

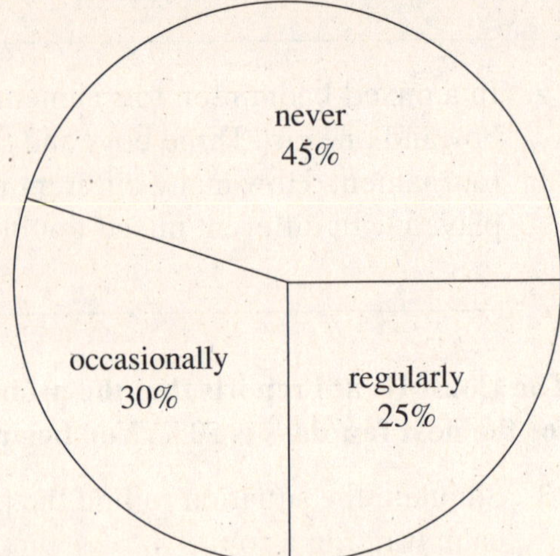

2. How many people responded in each of the categories?

   ____

   ____

3. What is the sample size?

   ____

4. Can you tell if the sample is random?

   ____

5. What type of sampling is used?

   ____

Explain why the survey questions in Exercises 6 and 7 are biased.

6. Would you rather buy the TV dinner with a picture of a luscious, gourmet meal on it, or one in a plain package?

   ____

7. Do you want your kids to receive a faulty education by having their school day shortened?

   ____

8. A researcher wants to find out what brand of tomato sauce is most popular with people who work full-time. He samples shoppers at a supermarket between 10 A.M. and 2 P.M. Is this a good sample? Explain.

   ____

   ____

9. You decide to run for student council. What factors are important to consider if you decide to survey your fellow students?

   ____

   ____

Practice 12-1

Sequences

Write the rule for each sequence and find the next three terms.

1. $3, 8, 13, 18,$ ___ , ___ , ___

2. $7, 14, 28, 56,$ ___ , ___ , ___

3. $32, 8, 2, \frac{1}{2},$ ___ , ___ , ___

4. $14, 11, 8, 5,$ ___ , ___ , ___

5. $35, 23, 11, -1,$ ___ , ___ , ___

6. $3{,}000, 300, 30, 3,$ ___ , ___ , ___

Find the next three terms in each sequence. Identify each as arithmetic, geometric, or neither. For each arithmetic or geometric sequence, find the common difference or ratio.

7. $7.1, 7.5, 7.9, 8.3,$ ___ , ___ , ___

8. $5, 6, 8, 11, 15, 20,$ ___ , ___ , ___

9. $8{,}000; 4{,}000; 2{,}000; 1{,}000;$ ___ ; ___ ; ___

10. $92, 89, 86, 83,$ ___ , ___ , ___

11. $-1, 2, -4, 8,$ ___ , ___ , ___

12. $2.3, 2.03, 2.003, 2.0003,$ ___ , ___ , ___

13. $1, 3, 6, 8, 16, 18, 36,$ ___ , ___ , ___

14. $140, 133, 126, 119,$ ___ , ___ , ___

15. $3, 9, 27, 81,$ ___ , ___ , ___

16. $540, 270, 90, 22.5,$ ___ , ___ , ___

Tell whether each situation produces an *arithmetic sequence*, *geometric sequence*, or *neither*.

17. The temperature rises at the rate of 0.75°F per hour. _______________

18. A person loses 2 lb each month. _______________

19. A toadstool doubles in size each week. _______________

20. A person receives a 6% raise each year. _______________

Find the first four terms of the sequence represented by each expression.

21. $4 \cdot 3^{n+1}$

22. $4 + 3(n-2)$

23. $n^2(n-1)$

Practice 12-2
Functions

Complete the table of input/output pairs for each function.

1. $y = 3x$

Input x	Output y
4	
8	
12	
16	

2. $z = 15n$

Input n	Output z
1	
2	
3	
	60

3. $d = 30 - s$

Input s	Output d
0	
5	
	20
	15

4. $h = 120 \div g$

Input g	Output h
2	
6	
	10
15	

5. $r = 2t - 1$

Input t	Output r
3	
9	
20	
	99

6. $p = 2v - 12$

Input v	Output p
	6
	40
43	
75	

Does each situation represent a function? Explain.

7. Input: the distance that needs to be biked

Output: the time it takes if you bike at 5 mi/h

____

8. Input: the time of day you go to the grocery store

Output: the cost of the groceries

____

9. Input: the number of copies of a book

Output: the total cost of the books

____

10. Input: a T-shirt color

Output: the T-shirt cost

____

Use the function rule $f(x) = 5x + 1$. Find each output.

11. $f(3)$　　**12.** $f(-6)$　　**13.** $f(8)$　　**14.** $f(-2)$

________　________　________　________

15. $f(1.5)$　　**16.** $f(25)$　　**17.** $f(30)$　　**18.** $f(100)$

________　________　________　________

Use the function rule $f(x) = 4n^2 - 1$. Find each output.

19. $f(0)$　　**20.** $f(1)$　　**21.** $f(-1)$　　**22.** $f(2)$

________　________　________　________

22. $f(-2)$　　**24.** $f(3)$　　**25.** $f(2.5)$　　**26.** $f(5)$

________　________　________　________

Practice 12-3

Graphing Linear Functions

Make a table of input/output pairs for each function. Then graph the function. Show only the portion that makes sense for each situation.

1. On a trip Alex averages 300 mi/day. The distance he covers (output) is a function of the number of days (input).

Input				
Output				

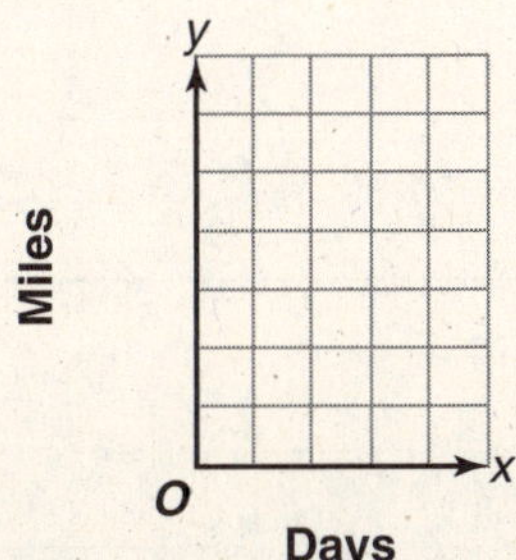

2. Suppose you earn $7 per hour. The number of hours you work (input) determines your pay (output).

Input				
Output				

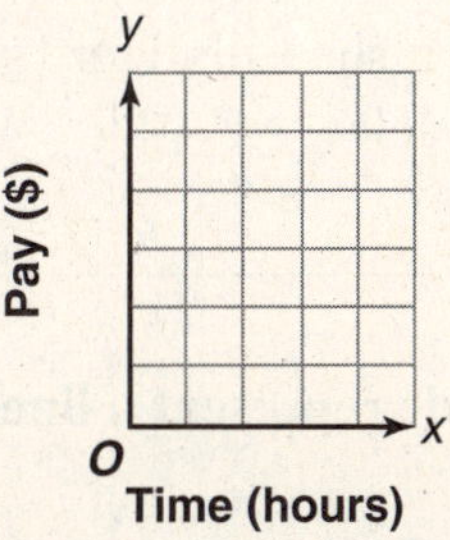

3. Suppose you have $50. The amount of money you spend (input) decreases the amount you have left (output).

Input				
Output				

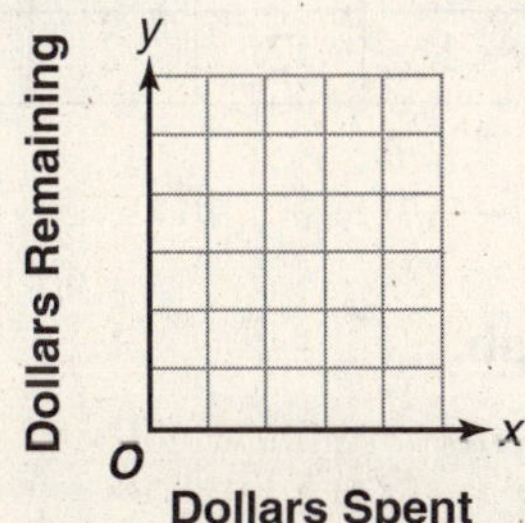

4. You have $10.00. Each week you save $2.50. The number of weeks you save (input) increases your savings (output).

Input				
Output				

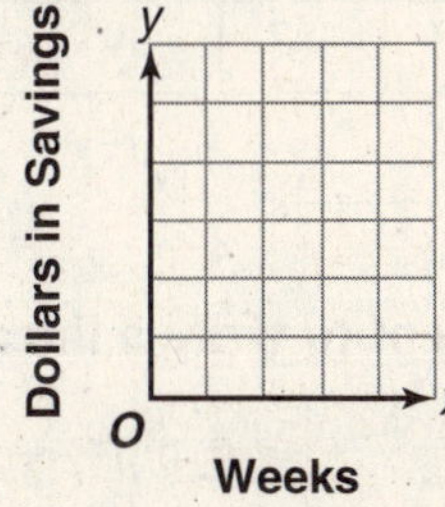

Graph each linear function.

5. $f(x) = -x + 4$

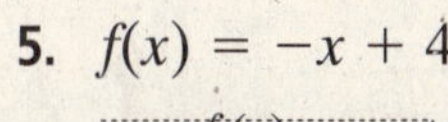
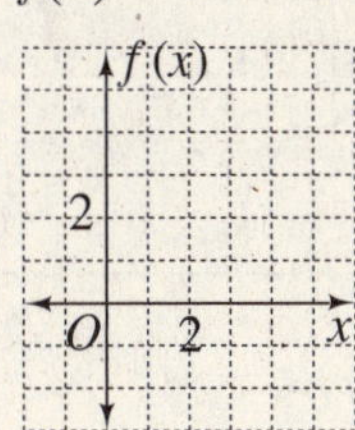

6. $f(x) = \frac{2}{3}x + 1$

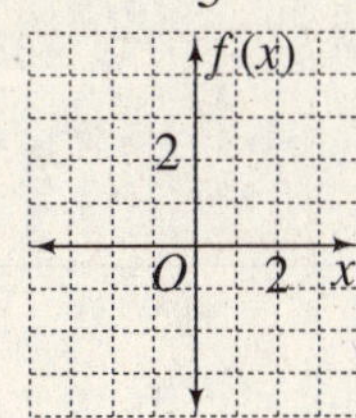

7. $f(x) = -2x + 1$

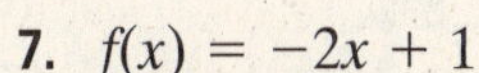
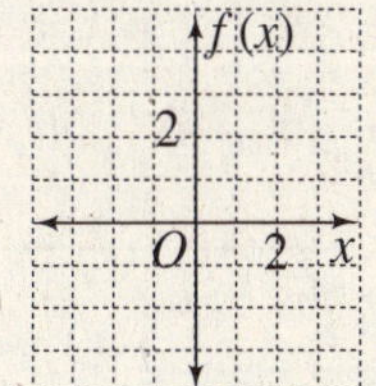

8. $y = -\frac{1}{2}x + 3$

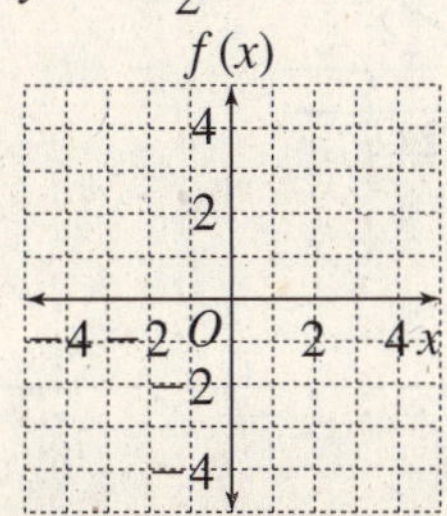

9. $y = -2 - 3x$

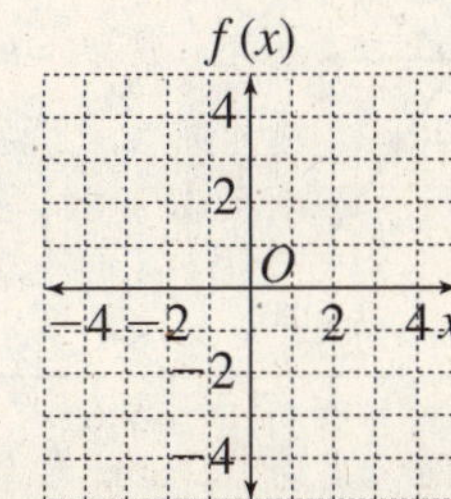

10. $y = 5 - 0.2x$

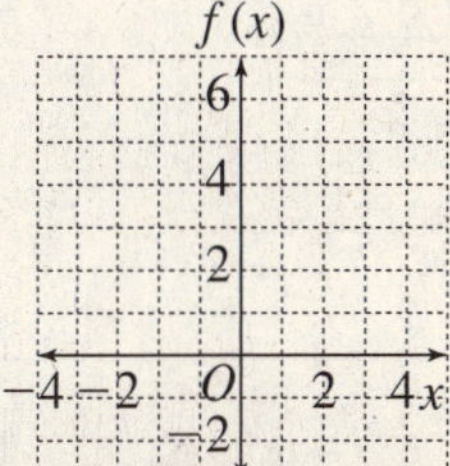

Practice 12-4   **Writing Rules for Linear Functions**

Write a linear function rule for each situation. Identify the input and output variables.

1. Amy sells tote bags at a craft fair for a day. She pays $50 to rent a booth. The materials and labor cost on each tote bag is $3.50. Her expenses for the day depend on how many tote bags she sells.

   ____

2. Ms. Watson receives a base pay of $150, plus a commission of $45 on each appliance that she sells. Her total pay depends on how many appliances she sells.

   ____

Does the data in each table represent a linear function? If so, write the function rule.

3.
Input	0	1	2	3	4
Output	2	5	8	11	14

4.
Input	0	1	2	3	4
Output	0	2	5	2	0

____

5.
Input	−2	0	4	6	8
Output	−1	−3	−7	−9	−11

6.
Input	−3	−2	−1	0	1
Output	−1	1	2	2	2

____

Use the slope and y-intercept to write a linear function rule for each graph.

7. 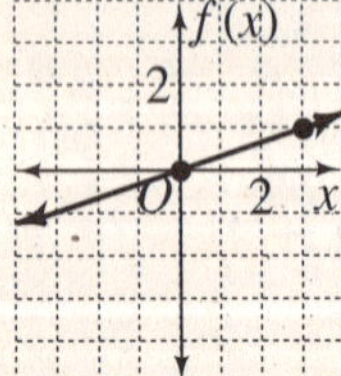

8. 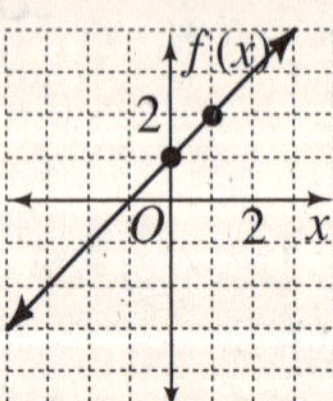

9. 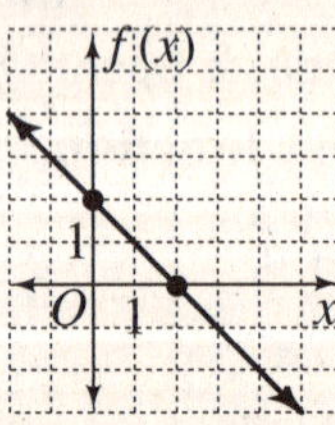

10. 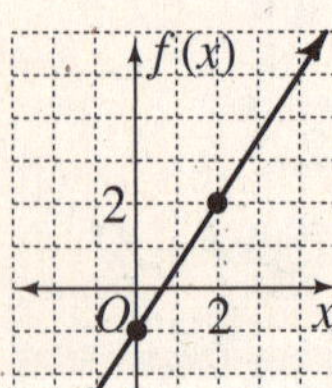

11. 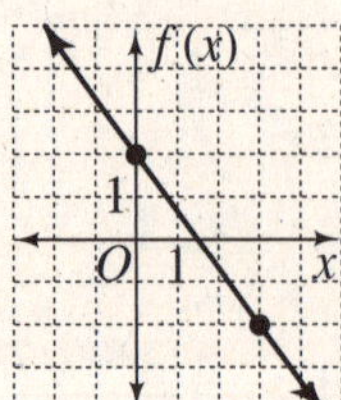

12. 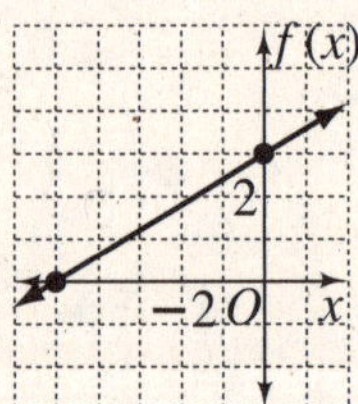

Practice 12-5

Relating Graphs to Events

Each graph represents a situation. Match a graph with the appropriate situation.

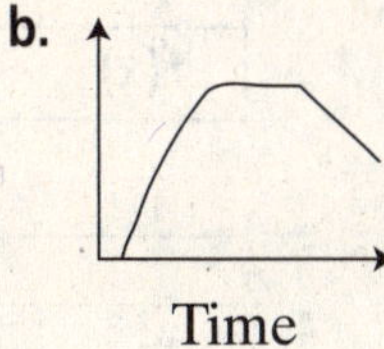

a.

Time

b.

Time

c.

Time

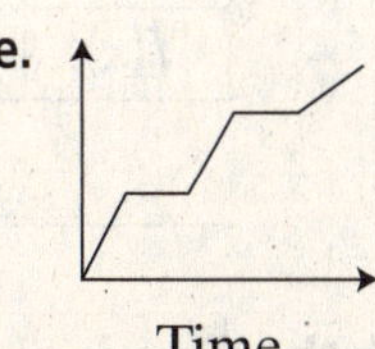

d.

Time

e.

Time

f.

Time

1. the amount of an unpaid library fine. ___________________

2. the height above ground of a skydiver during a dive. ___________________

3. one's adrenaline flow when receiving a fright. ___________________

4. the temperature of the air during a 24-h period beginning at 9:00 A.M. ___________________

5. oven temperature for baking cookies. ___________________

6. elevator ride up with stops. ___________________

Sketch and label a graph of each relationship.

7. The height of a football after it has been kicked

8. The distance traveled by a car that was driving 50 mi/h, but is now stopped by road construction

9. The function table at the right shows the distance in feet that an object falls over time.

Time (s)	Distance (ft)
1	16
2	64
3	144
4	256

Practice 12-6

Nonlinear Functions

Write a quadratic function rule for the data in each table.

1.

x	0	1	2	3	4
$f(x)$	3	4	7	12	19

____

2.

x	-2	-1	0	1	2
$f(x)$	-8	-2	0	-2	-8

____

3.

x	-1	0	1	2	3
$f(x)$	4	0	4	16	36

____

4.

x	-10	-5	0	5	10
$f(x)$	95	20	-5	20	95

____

Complete the table for each function. Then graph the function.

5. $f(x) = x^2 + 1$

x	$x^2 + 1 = f(x)$
-3	
-2	
-1	
0	
1	
2	
3	

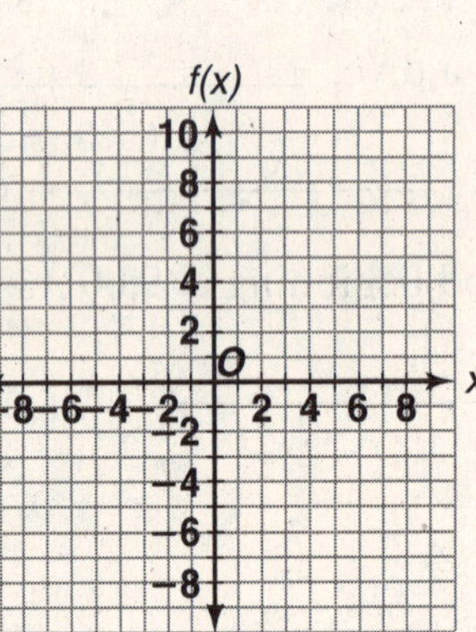

6. $f(x) = 4 - x^2$

x	$4 - x^2 = f(x)$
-3	
-2	
-1	
0	
1	
2	
3	

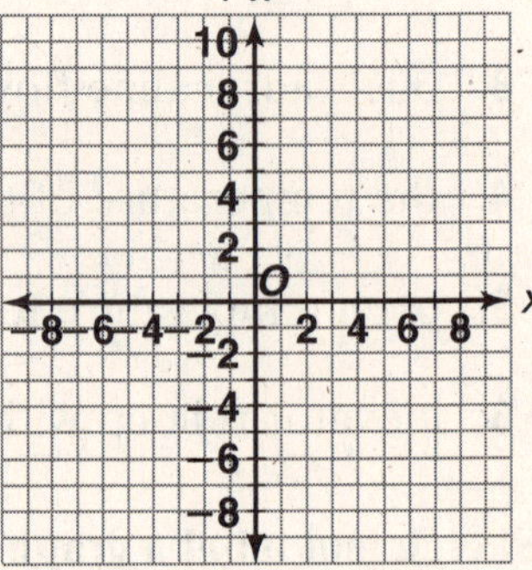

7. $f(x) = \dfrac{20}{x}$

x	$f(x)$
2	
4	
5	
10	

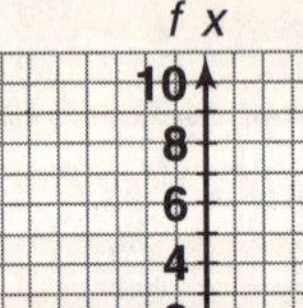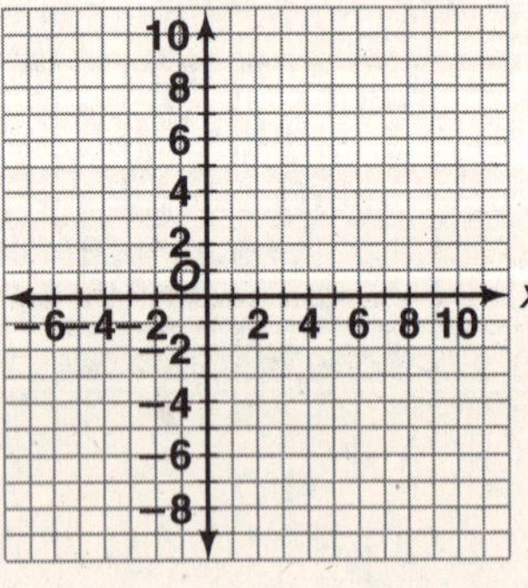

8. $f(x) = 2^x - 1$

x	$f(x)$
-1	
0	
1	
2	
3	

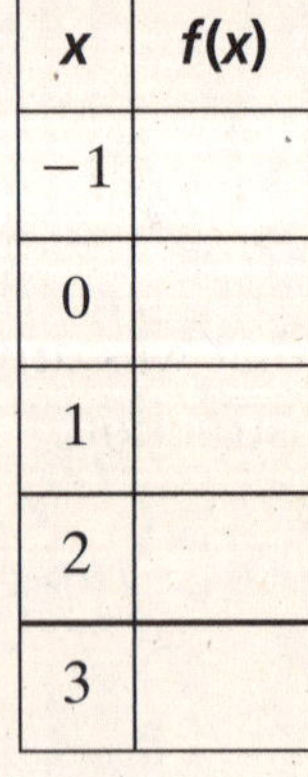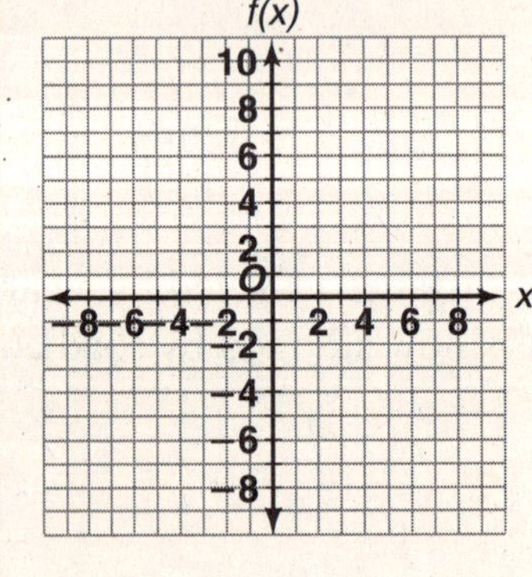

Does the point (2, 2) lie on the graph of each function?

9. $f(x) = 2x - 2$ **10.** $f(x) = \left(\dfrac{1}{2}\right)^x$ **11.** $f(x) = x^2 - x$ **12.** $f(x) = \dfrac{4}{x}$

_______________ _______________ _______________ _______________

Practice 12-7

Use any strategy to slove each problem. Show your work.

1. A population of 30 mice is released into a wildlife region. The population triples each year. Write a function rule that relates the number of mice to the amount of time that has passed. Use the rule to find the number of mice after 4 years and 8 years.

   ____

2. You bought a used car for $6,000. The value of the car will decrease 12% per year. So each year the car is 88% of the previous year's value. Write a function rule that relates the value of the car to the years that have passed. Use the rule to find the value of the car after 6 years.

   ____

3. The sum of two integers is -44. Their difference is 8. What are the two integers?

   ____

4. Margot earns $225 per week plus a commission of 2% on each appliance that she sells. Write a function rule that relates Margot's pay to the number of appliances that she sells. Use the rule to find her pay for a week in which she has sales of $15,234.

   ____

5. The cost of an international long distance phone call is $6.25 for the first minute and $3.75 for each additional minute. What was the total length of a call that cost $28.75?

   ____

6. A garden supply shop sells bags of topsoil. The bags come in six sizes: 16, 17, 23, 24, 39, and 40 pounds. The shop will not open or split bags. A greenhouse asks for 100 pounds of topsoil. Can the order be filled with bags in the sizes available? If not, how close can the supply shop come to filling the order?

   ____

Practice 12-8   **Exploring Polynomials**

In Exercises 1–5:

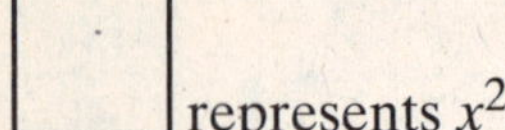 represents x^2,   represents x,   represents 1,

represents , $-x^2$ represents $-x$,   represents -1.

Write a variable expression for each model.

1. 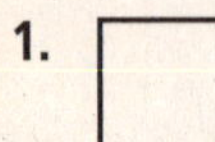

____

2. 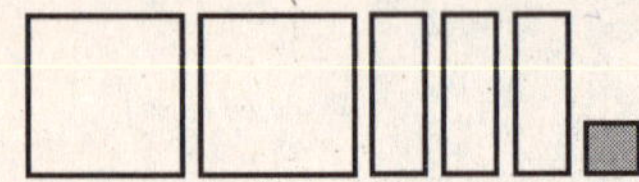

____

3. 

____

Write and simplify the polynomials represented by each model.

4. 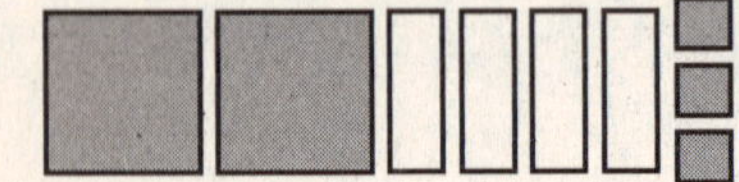

____

5. 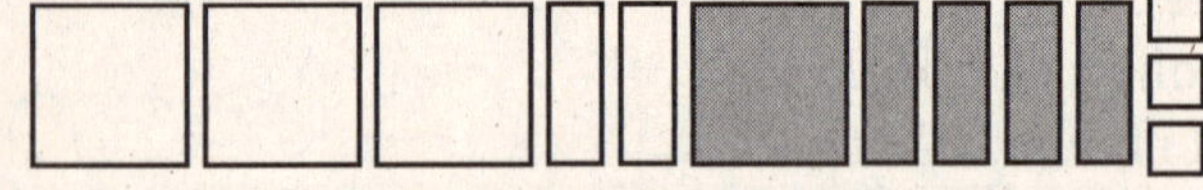

____

Simplify each polynomial.

6. $2x^2 - x^2 + 7x - 2x + 5$ **7.** $3x^2 + 2x - 8x + 6$

________________________   ________________________

8. $x^2 - 4x^2 + x + 5x - 8 + 3$ **9.** $x^2 + 6x + x^2 - 4x + 1 - 5$

________________________   ________________________

10. $3x^2 + 2x + 3x + 3 - 1$ **11.** $x^2 + 3x^2 + 3x - 9 + 2x$

________________________   ________________________

Practice 12-9

Adding and Subtracting Polynomials

Name the coefficients in each polynomial.

1. $x^2 - 3x + 5$

2. $b^2 - 4b + 3$

3. $-2a^2 + 4a - 6$

4. $x^3 - 2x^2 + 4x$

5. $14y^3 + 4y + 0$

6. $-11s^2 - 9s + 2$

Add.

7. $(5x - 4) + (6x + 2)$

8. $(3x^2 - 6x) + (x^2 + 2x)$

9. $(7x^2 + 3x - 5) + (-4x^2 - x + 4)$

10. $(x^2 - 2x) + (4x^2 + 7)$

11. $(2x^2 + 8) + (3x^2 - 9)$

12. $(7x^2 + 3x - 5) + (x^2 - 6x + 4)$

13. $(5x^2 - 3x + 3) + (4x - 5)$

14. $(3x^2 - 4x) + (2x^2 + x - 6)$

Find the perimeter of each figure.

15.

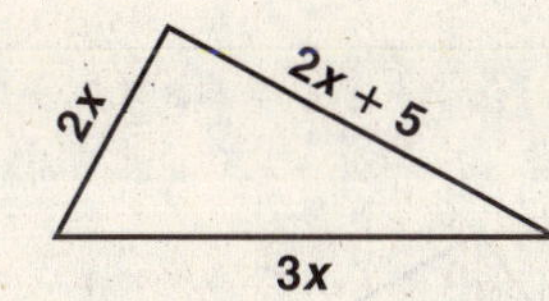

Subtract.

18. $(4x^2 + 1) - (x^2 + 3)$

19. $(2x^2 + 2x) - (8x + 7)$

20. $(3x^2 + 7x - 5) - (x^2 - 4x - 1)$

21. $(x^2 - 2x + 7) - (3x^2 - 9x + 2)$

22. $(6x^2 + 8x + 1) - (4x^2 - 8x + 7)$

23. $(4x^2 - 6x + 3) - (2x^2 - 7x - 9)$

Practice 12-10

Multiplying Polynomials

Find the area of each rectangle.

1. 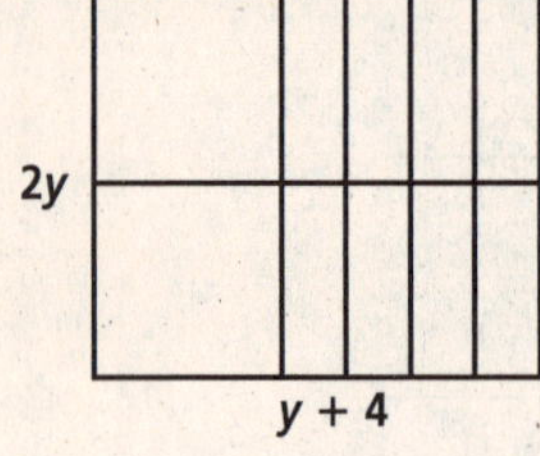

2. 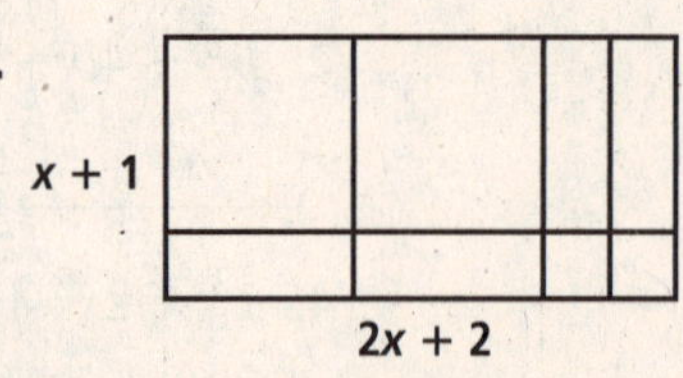

3. 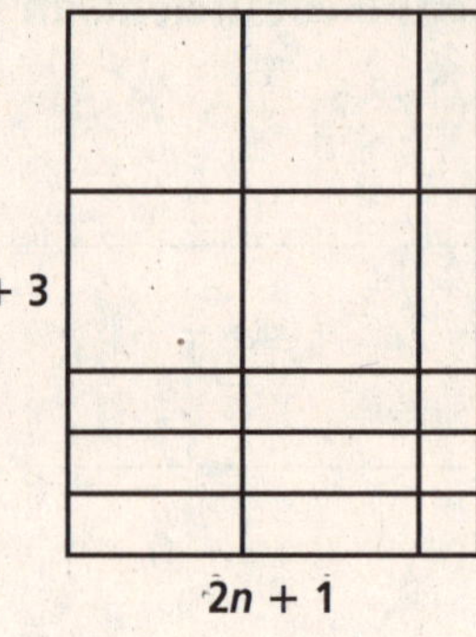

___________________   ___________________   ___________________

Simplify each expression.

4. $x^2 \cdot x^2$

5. $7x \cdot 2x$

6. $(-3t)t$

7. $(4x^2)(-2x)$

___________________   ___________________   ___________________   ___________________

8. $5m^2 \cdot 2m^2$

9. $(-x)(7x^2)$

10. $(3x^2)(-2x^3)$

11. $(-z)(-8z^2)$

___________________   ___________________   ___________________   ___________________

Use the Distributive Property to simplify each expression.

12. $x(x + 2)$

13. $3b(b - 5)$

14. $2x^2(x + 9)$

___________________   ___________________   ___________________

15. $2(a^2 + 8a + 1)$

16. $2x^2(4x + 1)$

17. $3l(l^2 + 4l - 6)$

___________________   ___________________   ___________________

Find the area of each figure.

18. 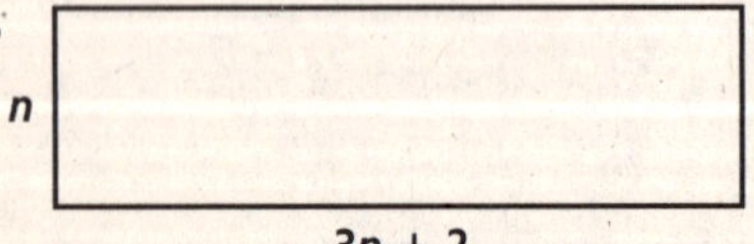

19. 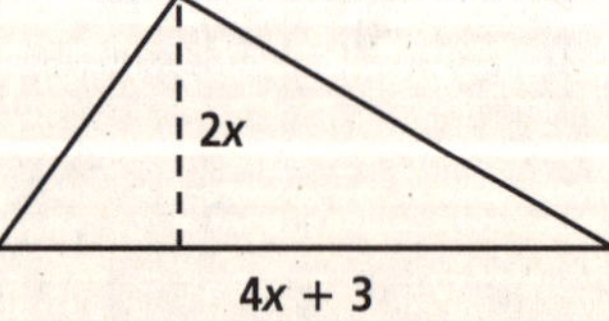

20. 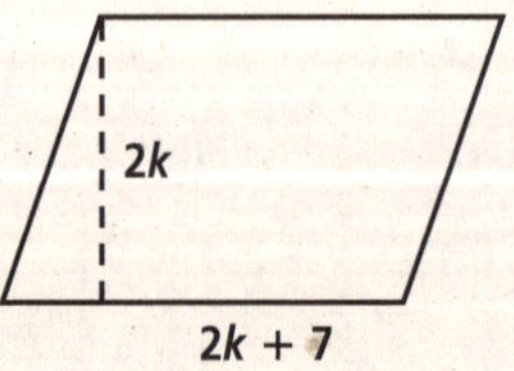

___________________   ___________________   ___________________

21. Multiply $4x$ by $-x^2 + 2x - 9$.

22. Multiply $-6x$ by $-2x^2 - 3x + 1$.

___________________   ___________________